START HERE...
the beginning point for starting a daily devotional life

Godspeed my friend!

BILL HURT

Bill Hurt

Psalm 23

WESTBOW
PRESS®
A DIVISION OF THOMAS NELSON
& ZONDERVAN

Copyright © 2019 Bill Hurt.

All rights reserved. No part of this book may be used or reproduced by any means, graphic, electronic, or mechanical, including photocopying, recording, taping or by any information storage retrieval system without the written permission of the author except in the case of brief quotations embodied in critical articles and reviews.

This book is a work of non-fiction. Unless otherwise noted, the author and the publisher make no explicit guarantees as to the accuracy of the information contained in this book and in some cases, names of people and places have been altered to protect their privacy.

WestBow Press books may be ordered through booksellers or by contacting:

WestBow Press
A Division of Thomas Nelson & Zondervan
1663 Liberty Drive
Bloomington, IN 47403
www.westbowpress.com
1 (866) 928-1240

Because of the dynamic nature of the Internet, any web addresses or links contained in this book may have changed since publication and may no longer be valid. The views expressed in this work are solely those of the author and do not necessarily reflect the views of the publisher, and the publisher hereby disclaims any responsibility for them.

Any people depicted in stock imagery provided by Getty Images are models, and such images are being used for illustrative purposes only.
Certain stock imagery © Getty Images.

Scripture taken from the King James Version of the Bible.

Scripture quotations marked (NIV) are taken from the Holy Bible, New International Version®, NIV®. Copyright © 1973, 1978, 1984, 2011 by Biblica, Inc.™ Used by permission of Zondervan. All rights reserved worldwide. www.zondervan.com The "NIV" and "New International Version" are trademarks registered in the United States Patent and Trademark Office by Biblica, Inc.™

ISBN: 978-1-9736-6474-1 (sc)
ISBN: 978-1-9736-6473-4 (hc)
ISBN: 978-1-9736-6475-8 (e)

Library of Congress Control Number: 2019907179

Print information available on the last page.

WestBow Press rev. date: 6/10/2019

I have chosen to dedicate this book to the body of believers at Pleasant Hill Baptist Church, Columbus, Mississippi. When I came to be your pastor, I was a broken man. You not only helped heal me, but you also saved my ministry. I will always be indebted to you.

START HERE...

Introduction

In 2009, I began writing daily devotional thoughts on social media. Never in a million years did I think it would lead to writing a book. Most of my writings dealt with what was going on in my life and ministry and our world. Along this journey, many friends and colleagues encouraged me to put my thoughts into print. What I did not know at the time was that many individuals were using these writings as a part of their daily devotions. That was both humbling and encouraging.

Over the years I have had so many people express their frustration at trying to develop a devotional life in their spiritual journey. After all, we live in such a fast-paced society that unfortunately God often draws the short end of the straw when it comes to our time. The reality of the Christian faith is: it is impossible to grow in our relationship with God if we do not spend time in prayer, Bible study, and reflection. We do not grow spiritually by osmosis.

This book, *Start Here*, is a beginning point for all those who want to start a daily quiet time with God. In this book, there are one hundred daily devotions along with a scripture passage for each day. It is my prayer that this book will help launch you into a daily time of communion with our Creator. The more you know Him, the more you will love Him. The more you love Him, the more you will want to serve Him. Start here and start now. Most of us could use a little quality time with the One who knows us the best and loves us despite ourselves.

Godspeed my friends.

START HERE...

Jesus – The Name Above All Names

There is one important fact that separates the Christian faith from all other religions. Our faith is not a memorial society built on the death of our fallen leader. The foundation of our faith is the resurrection of our Lord and Savior, Jesus Christ. When Muhammad died, he stayed dead, and his tomb remains sealed. When Confucius died, he stayed dead. When Buddha died, that was the end of his story. However, when Jesus of Nazareth was crucified and laid in a borrowed tomb, He rose from the dead on the third day and conquered death and hell. That is what makes our religion different from all the other religions of the world.

What began as a whisper in a graveyard over 2000 years ago, now reverberates all over the world as people from all walks of life celebrate the resurrection of our Lord. He is not just another religious figure who taught valuable life lessons. He is God's Son who took the sins of the world in His body and accepted the punishment for our transgressions. He did for us what we could never do for ourselves. That is what we celebrate each Sunday as we worship collectively as God's people. He not only makes the difference in this life but also in the life to come. The question you need to ask yourself this day is: "Do I know Him?"

"Salvation is found in no one else, for there is no other name under heaven given to mankind by which we must be saved" (Acts 4:12 NIV). "I am the way and the truth and the life. No one comes to the Father except through me" (John 14:6 NIV). It is time we live for the One who died for us. He does make a difference.

Godspeed my friends.

> *Therefore God exalted him to the highest place and gave him the name that is above every name, that at the name of Jesus*

every knee should bow, in heaven and on earth and under the earth, and every tongue acknowledge that Jesus Christ is Lord, to the glory of God the Father.

~Philippians 2:9-11 NIV

START HERE...

Overcoming Intentional Hurt

It is one thing to hurt another individual accidentally by word or deed. It is quite another to intentionally and calculatingly seek to hurt another. I do not think Simon Peter intentionally set out to hurt Jesus when he denied him three times. Judas, on the other hand, was deliberate in his plan to betray our Lord and Savior for thirty pieces of silver. The actions of both men were equally painful to their master. The difference: one deliberately and consciously performed the deed, and the other melted to the pressure of the moment and did what he never thought he would do.

We have had or been a part of situations like this in our lives. In my life, I have been the victim and the culprit. There have been times in my life when I have said or done something and had no clue it would hurt another. However, there have also been moments when I have said something or did something because I knew it would hurt another. When someone deliberately inflicts pain on another person, it is a clear indication that he is not walking closely with Christ. You cannot dispute that fact. The Christian faith is always about elevating others and never tearing them down.

Several years ago, I had a friend intentionally tell a lie about me. When confronted as to why he did it, his response was: "I did it to hurt you." What does one say and what does one do? Forgiveness was granted, but trust was never restored.

Over the years I have come to understand there are miserable, unstable, unhappy, and yes, evil people out there who love to inflict pain on other people. Allow me to let you in on a little secret. Some are in our churches. Our job is to forgive and to love and sometimes we must move on. We determine how long we will let another hold us captive by their actions. Once we forgive them, we move on, and wholeness begins. It may be your time to start the journey.

Godspeed my friends.

Do not repay evil with evil or insult with insult. On the contrary, repay evil with blessing, because to this you were called so that you may inherit a blessing.

~1 Peter 3:9 NIV

START HERE...

Nice People Sometimes Finish First

They say that nice guys finish last. Well, the Clemson University Tigers destroyed that theory last night when they, under the leadership of Dabo Swinney, won their second national championship during his tenure as head coach. Following the game, Swinney said: "All the credit – all glory – goes to the good Lord. Our keyword for the year was 'joy.' For me, joy comes from focusing on Jesus, others and yourself." In the high dollar days of college football, where sex scandals, abusive behavior, and recruiting violations are the norm, Swinney's program is different. The atmosphere is different. The culture is different. Oh, don't get me wrong; he has been scrutinized and investigated. However, do you know what the allegations were? His program was too religious and Christ-centered. Folks who are offended by his Christian stance have made these charges. It would be nice to have a few more coaches, teachers, preachers, lawyers, doctors, and other business people act in such an offensive way.

Last night as the clock ticked down, and the game concluded, even the most diehard Bama fans had a little glow in their hearts. What they will tell you is: "If we have to get beat, I'd rather get beat by Dabo." After all, he's a former Bama player, graduate, and coach. He's also one of Bama's favorite sons. After all, how can you not like Dabo? Oh, only those he offends with his faith dislike him. May his tribe increase.

Godspeed my friends.

> *I have told you this so that my joy may be in you and that your joy may be complete.*
>
> ~John 15:11 NIV

START HERE...

You Don't Know How They Feel

Sometimes, in our attempts to be sympathetic, empathetic, and comforting to others who are hurting, we utter five words that should never come out of our mouths: "I know how you feel." We make a false assumption that because we have had a similar situation, we know exactly how that person feels, and what they are experiencing. Friends, that is just not the case. Everyone is different.

First, not all relationships are equal. Let me give you an example. When my father died, I lost my Dad, mentor, pastor, compass, and best friend. When people would come up to me and say: "I know how you feel," I did not, but I wanted to say: "With all due respect, you do not have a clue as to how I feel." All relationships are different, and as individuals we are unique; how we process grief and loss is personal and different from others.

Second, it's hard to put into words how we feel as individuals, so why do we think we can speak as to the feelings others are experiencing? There are times that I don't know if I should laugh or cry due to the circumstances of my life. So, if I struggle with my thoughts and emotions, I surely do not need someone else to tell me they know what is going on in my head and heart.

So, what do you say or do? Well, you might want to say: "I have experienced a similar situation, but I cannot imagine your hurt." Sometimes just an embrace and a presence are enough to make a difference. Hurting people will not remember what you said, but they will remember if you were there. You do not have to say anything; your actions will express your love.

Godspeed my friends.

> *Carry each other's burdens, and in this way you will fulfill the law of Christ.*
>
> ~Galatians 6:2 NIV

START HERE...

Don't Forget to Remember

The ability to remember is a gift from God. Can you imagine what your life would be like if you had no memory? Every day would be a blank page, and even the simplest of tasks would be impossible to perform. Our memory helps us to live life repetitively and at the same time learn new skills. But as powerful and important as our memory is, it can also hold us back and destroy us.

I believe there are things we need to remember, but there are some things we need to forget. Just as your memory is a gift from God, so is your ability to forget certain things. The Apostle Paul wrote: "But one thing I do: Forgetting what is behind and straining toward what is ahead, I press on" (Philippians 3:13b-14a NIV). If you are going to live productively in the present, there are some things from the past you need to forget.

At the top of the list of things one needs to forget is our resentment towards others. Far too many folks are still walking around with resentment and anger towards others. We are angry over a word that someone said or a deed that someone performed against us in the past. Some of these things have frozen our hearts and prevented God from moving us forward. We may not be able to forgive and forget, but we can forgive and get on with life. Isn't it time to let go of a few things in life? When we do, we're ready to allow God to work in our lives in the present.

Godspeed my friends.

> *Forget the former things; do not dwell on the past. See, I am doing a new thing!*
>
> ~Isaiah 43:18-19a NIV

START HERE...

Running Through the Fog

The weather over the past few days has made it impossible to get outside and run. However, early this morning, I was determined to get in a few miles. As I made my way down the driveway, it started raining again. At that moment there was a call for a decision. Do we press on or turn back for the comfort and dryness of home? Well, the decision was made to forge ahead despite the conditions. It seemed like a good idea for the first twenty minutes. Then the rain got harder, and the wind blew colder. What did I do? I pressed on and finished.

There are moments in life when the conditions aren't optimal. There are days which are dark and cold; I'm not talking about outside, but rather inside. You reach a point where you wonder if life can get any blacker or harder. What do you do? You press on. Take a deep breath and remember a resource greater than your own strength is available. The presence of God may not remove the rough elements, but it can provide comfort during the difficult days. Rest assured, you can't hold back the dawn, and His light will eventually overtake the darkness.

I didn't run fast this morning, but I ran. I didn't run far this morning, but I ran. Sometimes all you can do in the rainy days of life is to move in the right direction regardless of the distance you may or may not cover. Just do something.

Godspeed my friends.

> *The light shines in the darkness, and the darkness has not overcome it.*
>
> ~John 1:5 NIV

START HERE...

Putting God Back in Our Homes

Throughout my lifetime there has been a cry to put God and the Bible back into our schools. I agree with this premise and recently had someone tell me about how mandatory chapel services at a Baptist college had a profound effect on his life. However, I think we're missing the main problem. Yes, our children need some spiritual nurturing during their formative years, but I think it needs to flow from a different source. We need to put God and the Bible back in our homes. If there's going to be a great spiritual awakening in our country, it won't start in our schools; it'll start in our homes and churches.

So, how is this possible? Well, for one thing, we need to remove the false gods we bring into our homes to bow down to and to worship. These gods may be the gods of leisure, prosperity, hobbies, and achievements. There's nothing wrong with these things when put in the proper order. However, the first commandment is: "You shall have no other gods before me" (Exodus 20:3 NIV).

Second, it's time to make God's word a priority. We'll spend hours surfing social media, but we won't spend fifteen minutes reading God's word. If you spend fifteen minutes a day reading God's word, you will read through the Bible in a year. Are you up for the challenge? My six-year-old great nephew has taken the challenge to read the New Testament in a year. What about you?

It's time to stop thinking that others are going to fix the spiritual mess we're in today. As a child of God, you have a chance to light the fire that can change our culture. Will you?

Godspeed my friends.

Unless the Lord builds the house, the builders labor in vain. Unless the Lord watches over the city, the guards stand watch in vain.
                                                    ~Psalm 127:1 NIV

START HERE...

Facing Death with Assurance

There is nothing more humbling and sacred than to stand next to someone who is dying. That person knows it, and so do you. The words that come out of your mouth are probably some of the most important you'll ever speak as eternity hangs in the balance. What do you say to someone who is about to cross over from this life into the next?

Yesterday, after finishing up a funeral service at the church, I got a text from a church member informing me that his father-in-law, who is not a member of our church, was in the final stages of his life. Of course, when you receive such information, time is of the essence. I went into the Intensive Care Unit and made my way to this man's room. His sweet daughter, who is a church member of mine, greeted me. I asked her if he knew the severity of the situation, and she said he did. Just then, her father opened his eyes and motioned for me to come to him. I simply said: "I know you've had better days, and you're about to have nothing but good days." He told me he was at complete peace and that he was looking forward to seeing his wife who had passed away three years earlier. This man was courageous and uplifting. I went on to say: "This is going to end well for you, but not for your family."

Listen closely: you will die just like you lived. If you have walked closely with your God, you will leave this world with grace, dignity, and courage. That's what I saw yesterday. May that be true of us all.

Godspeed my friends.

> *"Where, O death, is your victory? Where, O death, is your sting?" The sting of death is sin, and the power of sin is the law. But thanks be to God! He gives us the victory through our Lord Jesus Christ.*
>
> ~1 Corinthians 15:55-57 NIV

START HERE...

DNA Matters in a Church

While we were around the dinner table one night, my son-in-law asked me an interesting question: "What advice would you give to a young pastor?" Of course, my first answer was: "Run!!!" But after a little thought, I came back with the following response.

Every church has a unique DNA. The faster you understand that as a pastor, the better off you're going to be. The pastor's job is not to make the church into a model of a megachurch in a metropolitan city. The job of the pastor is to love the people and minister to them where they are. Also, there is still no better way to grow a church than by outreach. I still believe there's no substitute for sitting down with someone in their home and talking about their faith in Jesus. If I told you the number of folks we've added to our congregation over the last two years, you wouldn't believe it. That growth has come through outreach.

Finally, people are not looking so much for style as they are substance and authenticity in worship. I find it interesting, (and this is my opinion, so slow down on the stoning and the flogging) we've asked the world or the pagan what they want in a church; thus, the church looks more like the world rather than being an agent of change in the world. It's becoming harder and harder to be in the ministry. So young pastors, love God and grow in your relationship with Him, and love your people. It's simple, but many miss it.

Godspeed my friends.

> *And I tell you that you are Peter, and on this rock I will build my church, and the gates of Hades will not overcome it. I will give you the keys of the kingdom of heaven; whatever you bind on earth will be bound in heaven, and whatever you loose on earth will be loosed in heaven.*
> ~Matthew 16:18-19 NIV

START HERE...

Working the Puzzle of Life

Last night around nine o'clock, the girl cousins decided they wanted to work a jigsaw puzzle, so, the task of putting a 500-piece puzzle began. If you've ever undertaken such a task, you know the drill. First, you find all the edge pieces and start building the border of the puzzle. Second, you set the box up in such a manner that you can see how the picture looks. Third, you group the pieces in similar color patterns to make the work easier. Then you are ready to start.

As you work as a team, the task becomes easier. However, it's also frustrating when you can't find that certain piece that completes an all-important section. After a while, everything starts looking the same. But then, suddenly, one piece leads to two; then two, to three. As the picture starts to come into focus, and the pieces become fewer, the work gets faster. We completed the work in a little over an hour. At times it was fun, while other times were slow and difficult. That, my friend, is a parable of life.

As we try to put the pieces of our lives together, the work becomes difficult and frustrating. It's hard to see how certain pieces of our lives fit together. Why did this event take place and why did we suffer such heartache? However, God, the Master Puzzle Solver, knows how every piece fits together. He does not need to find the edge pieces first, and He certainly does not need the box. He sits down, and without hesitation, He says: "This piece goes here. That piece goes there." He continues until the puzzle is complete.

Here's the good news. One day, not today, but one day, you'll sit in His presence and say: "Oh! Now I understand." Paul said it this way: "For now we see only a reflection as in a mirror; then we shall see face to face. Now I know in part; then I shall know fully, even as I am fully known" (1 Corinthians 13:12 NIV) You will understand how every piece of the puzzle fits together and how God was working in the background to bring about good.

    Godspeed my friends.

> *And we know that in all things God works for the god of those who love him, who have been called according to his purpose.*
>
> *~Romans 8:28 NIV*

START HERE...

How We React

The other day I dropped into Chick-fil-A for a quick bite to eat at lunchtime. As I got out of my car and took one step, my foot landed on a half-filled plastic water bottle. The bottle top was probably not secure because what happened next is something I have never seen before. The pressure of my foot on that bottle caused an explosion of water that soaked the back of my pants, my shoes, and socks. Now if you know anything about me, I might be a little picky about my clothes. I happened to be wearing light grey slacks, so there was no hiding the mess.

The first thought that ran through my mind was: "What selfish, inconsiderate, half-wit, ill-mannered low life would litter a parking lot?" There was no need to go full-blown Clark Griswold about the situation, and then ask for the Tylenol. Then in a moment of clarity, a rational thought came to mind. "In the grand scheme of things, how big is this?" After all, it was just water, and I could wash the pants.

Charles Swindoll said: "I am convinced that life is 10 percent what happens to me and 90 percent how I react to it." Far too often in my life, I allow small things to have a big effect on my life. George Carlin, who was not so religious, reminded us: "Don't sweat the petty things, and don't pet the sweaty things." Now those are words by which we should live. Watch out for half-filled water bottles; they can make a mess.

Godspeed my friends.

> *Better a patient person than a warrior, one with self-control than one who takes a city.*
>
> ~Proverbs 16:32 NIV

START HERE...

Secure Your Mask First

Are you trying to carry a load that's entirely too large or heavy? Amid grief and sorrow, are you so busy trying to take care of everybody else that you've forgotten to take care of yourself? Now you find yourself amid confusion and uncertainty. The tasks that once were so easy now have become difficult. Life seems to speed up in the day and slow down at night. You find yourself about to crash, and you do not know why. Where do you turn and what do you do?

Have you ever been on a plane and really listened to the flight crew explain what to do in case of an emergency. If there's a certain drop in altitude, the oxygen mask will drop down in front of you. The instructions are as follows: "Secure your mask first, then help others who need assistance." In other words, you're no good to anyone if you haven't taken care of yourself. However, in life, we're usually the last people we take care of during difficult days.

When the burden becomes too heavy, talk to someone you can trust. You'll never know what a difference a sympathetic ear will do. Second, talk to God. Why? Well, the answer lies in a song we used to sing. "Jesus loves me this I know, for the Bible tells me so. Little ones to him belong; they are weak, but he is strong." His strength can make all the difference.

Godspeed my friends.

> *Take my yoke upon you and learn from me, for I am gentle and humble in heart, and you will find rest for your souls. For my yoke is easy and my burden is light.*
> ~Matthew 11:29-30 NIV

START HERE...

Don't Be So Sensitive

When I was a child, and something hurt my feelings or offended me, my parents taught me that everyone is entitled to an opinion. They also taught me that it's necessary sometimes to put on your big boy pants and deal with it. However, they never taught me to be disrespectful or obnoxious. As a matter of fact, my Dad always told me: "There are only so many hills you can die on in life. Die on the ones that matter." In other words, he was telling me that I'd cut my life short by exhausting my efforts on little things in life that don't matter.

I'm constantly amazed today at what offends some individuals. "Rudolph the Red-Nosed Reindeer" is now offensive. "Baby It's Cold Outside" is now offensive. But what's not offensive is interrupting a political figure's dinner or breakfast in a public place with vulgar words and unnecessary hate. What's not offensive is a high school band portraying the killing of law enforcement officers during a halftime program. What's not offensive is degrading the highest office in the land each night on talk shows. What's not offensive is the removal of everything that might suggest Jesus during the Christmas season.

Oh, but I know what some will say. We are guaranteed free speech. Well, that applies to everyone, even the Christians of the world. This is a hill upon which we must be willing to die. This Christmas season will you speak a word for Christ? Remember, don't chase crazy, you'll never catch it.

Godspeed my friends.

Fools show their annoyance at once, but the prudent overlook an insult.

~Proverbs 12:16 NIV

START HERE...

R-E-S-P-E-C-T

I don't mind if you disagree with me politically. That's what makes our country great. We don't have to agree on everything theologically. That's why we have different denominations. (However, there are some non-negotiables of the Christian faith.) We don't have to agree on every social issue. That's why there are opinions. But, when it comes to lack of respect, that's where I draw the line. One of the biggest problems in our society is the lack of respect we have for authority.

There was a time I enjoyed watching late night talk shows, but that is a thing of the past for me. The reason is quite simple: the narrative is the same night after night. I get so tired of listening to them constantly bash the President of the United States. There is zero respect for the highest office in our country. And, just for the record, I felt the same way when our last president was in office. However, if you think he was treated the same by the press as our current president and the president before him, you need to pull your head out of the sand. There was and is a double standard.

The lack of respect is not limited to politics, but it bleeds over into our schools and even our churches. No longer are children afraid of their teachers and coaches. There is no need to be because Momma and Daddy will always go to bat for them. The same is true in the church. Things that are said to ministers today would blow your mind. There are times when I think my Dad would last about a week in the ministry due to the lack of respect given to the position today.

There are a lot of things which could be changed in our culture if we had what Aretha sang about so many years ago: RESPECT. We need mutual respect for one another regardless of race, gender, creed, or color. Love and respect can cover a multitude of sins. Maybe it's time to start.

Godspeed my friends.

Slaves, in reverent fear of God submit yourselves to your masters, not only to those who are good and considerate, but also to those who are harsh.

~1 Peter 2:18 NIV

START HERE...

Please Don't Ignore Me!

Most of us can handle a lot of things in life but being ignored isn't one of them. It doesn't matter if it's the salesclerk, the teacher, the boss, a friend, or even a family member. To have another not respond to us can be one of the most frustrating and degrading things that can happen in life. We want, and sometimes need, to hear a response to our question, statement or even argument. I know it's true in my life. If you really want to set me off, just ignore me.

As bad as it is when another individual stiffs us or ignores us, it's even worse when we feel as though God has turned a deaf ear towards our request. We pray and pray and Heaven seems to be made of brass. Our words seem to bounce off the ceiling and come back right back to us. We wonder at times if God hears us or even cares about our situation. Remember this simple truth: a prayer that God does not immediately answer does not mean He has not heard it. God knows what you need even before you ask. However, he does not respond in our time, nor answer our prayers according to our will. Can you even imagine what your life would be like if you got everything you prayed for over the years?

When you pray, be assured that God is not ignoring you. However, because God loves and cares for you, He answers your requests according to His time and His will. It's hard to understand all of this right now, but one day you'll see how every piece of the puzzle of your life fits together for good (Romans 8:28). It's called trusting God and not trying to figure it all out on your own. He cares more than you'll ever know on this earth.

Godspeed my friends.

> *I cried out to him with my mouth; his praise was on my tongue.*
> *If I had cherished sin in my heart, the Lord would not have*
> *listened; but God has surely listened and has heard my prayer.*
> ~Psalm 66:17-19 NIV

START HERE...

One Step at a Time

Over the years I have had people ask me why I love running so much. Well, let's clarify something from the start; I don't love running, even though I have been doing it for about twenty years. I love playing golf. I love riding bikes. I love eating a good steak. But running and I have a love/hate relationship. I hate getting started, but I love how I feel when I finish. I have always said: "I run so I can eat what I want when I want." Of course, ice cream is at the top of that list.

However, there are certain aspects of running that move me physically, emotionally, and, sometimes, even spiritually. There are moments during a run when my body is aching so much that I feel I can't take another step. Something miraculous happens. Not only do I take another step, but I take another, and another, and then another. The mind motivates and stimulates the body to do things it doesn't believe it can. Before you know it, one mile becomes two, and two becomes five. All this takes place while the body believes it can't do it.

The same is true with life. We all have to admit there are moments when we think we can't face another minute or hour, much less another day. At that very moment, a quiet voice whispers: "Take one step at a time. You can do this. I'm with you every step of the way." Before you know it, one day becomes two, and two becomes a week, and a week becomes a month, all due to a power that goes beyond yourself. The presence of God in the race of life is the difference in making it or quitting it. Don't stop; keep moving. It's not easy, but the joy at the end will be worth it.

Godspeed my friends.

Therefore do not worry about tomorrow, for tomorrow will worry about itself. Each day has enough trouble of its own.
~Matthew 6:34 NIV

START HERE...

When Does Life Begin?

Yesterday, we had the opportunity to go with our youngest daughter, Melanie, who is expecting our first grandchild, to her sonogram. I am not sure we would have wanted our parents to go with us, but it was one of my highest honors of all time.

As the technician was working her magic, suddenly I saw LIFE, not just any life, but the life of my grandchild. I saw both feet moving and often dancing. I saw little hands that will one day hold my hands. I saw a spine, from top to bottom. Finally, I saw a face with both eyes at the same time looking right at me. I saw the future just for a moment, and it looked great. The technician told us that our baby weighs about ten ounces and that everything looks fine. As for the gender, we'll find that out tomorrow. You know, these days, you have a reveal party, and we're no different.

I know there's a big argument as to when life begins; some say at birth, while others say at conception. Others will say life begins when the dog dies, and the kids move out. As for me, I'm pro-life; always have been and always will be. While still in his mother's womb, Jeremiah was called by God "Before I formed you in the womb I knew you, before you were born I set you apart; I appointed you as a prophet to the nations" (Jeremiah 1:5 NIV). If that is when my Lord believes life begins, that's good enough for me.

Godspeed my friends.

> For you created my inmost being; you knit me together in my mother's womb. I praise you because I am fearfully and wonderfully made; your works are wonderful, I know that full well. My frame was not hidden from you when I was made in the secret place, when I was woven together in the depths of the earth. Your eyes saw my unformed body; all the days ordained for me were written in your book before one of them came to be.
> ~Psalm 139:13-16 NIV

START HERE...

Facing Life's Storms

Early Tuesday morning, around two o'clock, I was awakened by the sound of sirens notifying us that we were under a tornado warning. I got out of the bed and lay down in the hallway until the storm had passed. The next day, while driving to a meeting, I noticed how beautiful the day was. The sky was crystal blue with the absence of any clouds. If I didn't know better, it would have been impossible to know that less than ten hours earlier, people in our area were facing a serious, maybe even a life-changing, event. That's how quickly the weather and life can change.

I believe there are three types of people in life: those in a storm, those coming out of a storm, and those about to go through a storm. Life, like the weather, is often unpredictable. With the least amount of warning, our whole world as individuals can be changed. Before we know it, a loved one of ours dies unexpectedly. After running a series of test, a doctor informs us we have cancer. Without notice, a relationship changes for the worst. All of a sudden, the windows of our souls begin to shake, and these frail vessels which we live in take a beating. Just at that moment when the storm seems unending, a voice quietly speaks: "Peace be still, I'm here."

The presence of God may not remove the storm altogether, but He takes the helm of our ships and navigates us home. His light shines in the darkness, and the darkness cannot comprehend it. In other words, no matter how dark the night, you can't hold back the dawn. Take His hand and let Him guide you safely home.

Godspeed my friends.

Be strong and courageous. Do not be afraid or terrified because of them, for the Lord your God goes with you; he will never leave you nor forsake you.

~Deuteronomy 31:6 NIV

START HERE...

Small Things Can Make Loud Noises

One Friday evening, we were driving to a local restaurant for dinner when suddenly we heard an awful noise coming from under the car! It sounded like a chain dragging. When we parked, I looked under the car for a limb, a dangling piece of metal or an actual chain. I saw nothing that could have been responsible for that noise.

After we ate, a friend of mine got in the car and immediately said: "You have a small rock that has gotten between your brake pads and is rolling around making this noise." He assured me that, eventually, it would work its way out. This thing had to be a boulder because by Monday it was still there. My youth pastor, David Honeycutt, took my car to his shop yesterday and within minutes, he found the culprit. It was a small pebble, no bigger than your fingernail on your pinky finger. Such a small object made a big noise.

That's a parable about life. Sometimes small things cause the biggest problems in our lives. They make the biggest noise, which pulls our attention from the important things in life. The same is true in our spiritual life. Often, it's not the big sins that trip us up, but the small things, which, after a while, become bigger and louder. For many of us, if we would take care of the little things, the big things would fall right in place. What's true with a small rock in the wheel of a car is true with life. It's a great relief when the noise finally ceases.

Godspeed my friends.

> *Therefore, since we are surrounded by such a great cloud of witnesses, let us throw off everything that hinders and the sin that so easily entangles. And let us run with perseverance the race marked out for us, fixing our eyes on Jesus, the pioneer and perfecter of faith.*
>
> ~Hebrews 12:1-2a NIV

START HERE...

Little Acts of Kindness Aren't Always Forgotten

The other night, while attending a funeral visitation in Canton, MS, I had a young man approach me. The closer he got to me, the more I knew that our paths had crossed; but I could not put a name with the face. Of course, this is a sure sign of old age. He came up to me and identified himself. You see, his parents were members of our church in Canton, but he wasn't. He went on to say: "I'll never forget the time you came to the emergency room and stayed with me and prayed with me following my tractor accident. I just wanted to tell you how much that meant at the time and to say thank you for being there." Now, you need to realize that this accident occurred about twenty years ago.

As he walked away, I was stunned. Twenty years after the fact he remembered something I had done, and to be quite honest, I vaguely remember the incident. However, it was still fresh on his mind. There are two quick lessons I want you to consider today.

First, so often in life, it's not the big things we do which have the greatest impact on others but rather the small seemingly insignificant things. You'll never know when an embrace, visit, or a word of encouragement will make a huge difference in someone's life. That small gesture can often be the difference in a person making it or not.

Second, it's never too late to tell someone "thank you." Karl Barth said: "All sin is simply ingratitude." Maybe you and I need to say "thanks" to someone who has had an impact on our lives. It could be a parent, a teacher, a minister, a coach or a mentor to whom you need to express your gratitude this day. You'll never know what small deed will make a huge difference in another's life.

Godspeed my friends.

> *Be kind and compassionate to one another, forgiving each other, just as in Christ God forgave you.*
>
> *~Ephesians 4:32 NIV*

START HERE...

Know Your Role

The other day, my daughter and her husband asked me to go with them to look for a new car. They had narrowed their choices to a couple of vehicles. For over a month they had researched all the different types of SUV's and had settled on a particular model, year, and mileage range. They decided that a low-mileage used car would fit their needs. They had saved a down payment, been to their credit union and gotten pre-approved; now they were ready to pull the trigger. If you were going to do this by the book, they did it. However, there was one thing that puzzled me. Why was I there? They certainly didn't need me, because they had already done everything to perfection.

When it came down to the final price, my son-in-law turned to me and asked: "Do you think we're getting a good deal?" Now my role was becoming crystal clear. All they needed was a little assurance that they had done a good job. I told him: "Tell them to throw in a bug guard and all-weather floor mats, and they've got a deal!"

You see, I know you'll find this hard to believe because I'm such a go-along-to-get-along, non-opinionated type of individual. There were moments when I wanted to tell them a few things, but that's not my job. Too often as parents, we never let our adult children become adults. They grow and learn through difficult times. You can't always swoop in and make everything nice and easy. Let them do and experience life.

They got the car, and I told them I was so proud of them. I'm no longer "the guy" in my daughter's life, and I'm okay with that. She's in good hands. Now if I can only get them to pick up the ticket for dinner occasionally. Nope, I will gladly pay that while I can.

Godspeed my friends.

"Haven't you read," he replied, "that at the beginning the Creator 'made them male and female,' and said, 'For this reason a man will leave his father and mother and be united to his wife, and the two will become one flesh'?"

~Matthew 19:4-5 NIV

START HERE...

Changing Our Perspective

Sometimes in life, it helps to get a little perspective on your current situation. There's a big difference in a problem and an inconvenience. Let me give you an example to explain my point. In August 2005, Hurricane Katrina, a category five storm, slammed the gulf coast of Mississippi and New Orleans, leaving thousands among thousands homeless. At First Baptist Church, Natchez, where I served as pastor, we housed over three hundred individuals when our family life center became a Red Cross shelter. These people had lost everything. In other words, they were facing a real problem.

At the same time, due to the high winds, our house was without electricity. We were forced to move in with one of our church members. What we would normally view has a major ordeal was now just a minor inconvenience. There is a huge difference in losing your home and losing your electricity.

The same is true in our own lives. A minor inconvenience comes our way, and we feel like we have been hit by a major hurricane when, in reality, we haven't even gone through a thunderstorm. Sometimes a little perspective will help us understand that we don't have it quite so bad. If you're throwing a temper tantrum over a small issue, give me a call one day and accompany me to one of our hospitals. You will quickly see you don't have it quite so bad.

Godspeed my friends.

Set your minds on things above, not on earthly things.
~Colossians 3:2 NIV

START HERE...

More Than a Feeling

There are moments in my life when I don't feel like a Christian. There, now I have said it. However, my faith isn't based on how I feel, but rather whom I know. If you were honest, I would imagine you have felt the same way. Don't worry or panic and start thinking you are a heathen. As a matter of fact, rather than considering yourself abnormal, rest assured, if you've had those moments of doubts and aloneness as a child of God, take a deep breath; you're more normal than you think.

When one examines some of the great heroes of our faith, we see they experienced times of doubt, isolation, and fear. These individuals questioned their faith, their calling, and even God. Jeremiah asked God: "Will you be like a deceitful brook to me?" John the Baptist, who baptized Jesus, sent a message to the Lord asking: "Are you the one or should we look for another?" Now if these two had those moments of doubt, what does that say about you and me.

Listen very carefully: my grasp on God isn't nearly as important as his grasp on me. In those moments when I don't feel close to Him, one thought returns to my mind: "He hasn't moved." Maybe I need to slide a little closer to His arms and allow Him to navigate my life through the waters I have disturbed. Remember, it's not how you feel, but whom you know.

Godspeed my friends.

> *For it is by grace you have been saved, through faith—and this is not from yourselves, it is the gift of God— not by works, so that no one can boast.*
>
> ~Ephesians 2:8-9 NIV

START HERE...

The Statue of Limitations on Forgiveness

Over the past few weeks, we have heard a lot of opinions about whether or not a person should be held accountable for something they did years ago. I have gone on the record and said that if the public knew everything I ever did, I'm not sure I'd be in the ministry today. But my life and many others are prime examples that God can use imperfect vessels to accomplish great things for His kingdom. In other words, our failures in life do not have to be final.

But, for just a moment, I want you to think about the concept of holding one accountable for things they may or may not have done in the past. I have seen this played out in the church in my thirty-plus years of ministry. Someone holds a grudge against another person based on an action or word from years ago. As a result, a heart has grown bitter and cold when it comes to forgiveness. But, the funny thing that I have noticed is that many of those same people have screamed at the top of their lungs for a month that you can't hold someone responsible for things that happened thirty years ago. The door of forgiveness must swing both ways.

Always keep in mind that the manner in which we forgive others is the same standard God uses on us. You can't scream one thing out of your mouth and hold the opposite in your heart. Unfortunately, too many church folks have done just that. The sad part? It damages the Kingdom of God. I thought our purpose was to advance it, not bring it to a screeching halt. Just give it a little thought and be consistent.

Godspeed my friends.

> *For if you forgive other people when they sin against you, your heavenly Father will also forgive you. But if you do not forgive others their sins, your Father will not forgive your sins.*
> ~Matthew 6:14-15 NIV

START HERE...

Live Like You Are Dying

If you knew you only had one year to live, would your priorities be the same, or would they be a bit different? Tim McGraw recorded a song several years ago which suggested we live like we were dying. You do realize that death is closer to you today than it has ever been. In other words, you need to live like you're dying because you are. Sooner or later everybody dies.

The Bible is a book about life, but it also addresses the subject of death quite often. It talks about the necessity to be prepared for the inevitable. Now at this moment, I know what many of you are thinking: "I don't like hearing all this stuff about death." Okay, we'll drop the subject when people stop dying. The moment you come into this world you begin a journey towards death. So, if that's the truth, where are your priorities in life? Treat this day as if it were your last, and you'll be surprised at the beauty and majesty you'll find. Stop majoring on the minor and close your book of complaints on the world. Rejoice in the fact that you have a gift in this day.

The Psalmist said: "This is the day which the Lord hath made; we will rejoice and be glad in it" (Psalm 118:24 KJV). If God made this day, and you are His child, then take a moment and be thankful. Today may be the only opportunity you have.

Godspeed my friends.

> *But our citizenship is in heaven. And we eagerly await a Savior from there, the Lord Jesus Christ, who, by the power that enables him to bring everything under his control, will transform our lowly bodies so that they will be like his glorious body.*
>
> ~Philippians 3:20-21 NIV

START HERE...

Do You Really Want to be Healed?

In the 5th chapter of John's gospel, there is a story that has always fascinated me. There was a man who had been an invalid for 38 years. When Jesus stubbles across this individual and sees his condition, he asks him: "Do you want to be healed?" I always thought that was an interesting question. Of course, he wanted to be healed, who wouldn't? Or did he? You see, if healing took place, everything in his life would change. He would have to get a job and provide for himself. He would have to find a place to live. He would not have others taking care of him. He would be on his own. Did he really want to be healed?

The same is true for some of us today. There are people out there who take great joy in their misery. They have grown accustomed to their pain and sorrow. They have no interest in being healed because they are afraid of the necessary steps it will take to be healthy. After all, if healing takes place, they will no longer be the center of attention. Changes will be required.

I believe that Jesus is asking the same question to some of us. Do you want to be healed? It may take a visit to the doctor. Talking to a counselor or your pastor may be part of the healing process. It might require a bit of forgiveness on your part. Aren't you tired of wallowing in self-pity? Don't you want to feel whole again? Jesus doesn't say: "You made your bed, now lie in it." No, to the contrary, he says: "Get up! Pick up your mat and walk" (John 5:8 NIV). But only if you want to get well.

Godspeed my friends.

> *When Jesus saw him lying there and learned that he had been in this condition for a long time, he asked him, "Do you want to get well?" "Sir," the invalid replied, "I have no one to help me into the pool when the water is stirred. While I am trying to get in, someone else goes down ahead of me."*
>
> ~John 5:6-7 NIV

START HERE...

Skeletons in Our Closets

In late 1991 I went in view of a call to become the pastor of First Baptist Church, Canton, Mississippi. At some point during that weekend, I gave my testimony. I told the congregation: "If this works out, and I become your pastor, there will be a time when you're involved in a conversation with some people about the church. The question will come up, 'Who is your pastor?' When you reply, 'Bill Hurt,' someone is going to nearly choke to death, because they knew me from my college days. They will say, 'Bill Hurt? Man, I never dreamed he'd be a minister. You should have seen all the things he once did. I'm not sure he's minister material." I went on to tell the church: "I haven't always been a preacher. You need to know that."

We all have skeletons in our closets. No matter who you are, there are things you've done that bring back shame and guilt; not just you, but, remember, some of the greatest heroes of our faith failed miserably. They were imperfect vessels that God used. Moses was a murderer. David was an adulterer. Elijah suffered greatly from depression. And the Apostle Paul, well, don't get me started on him. The good news about the gospel of Jesus Christ is that God is more concerned about where a person is right now, rather than where they were eighteen years ago.

There is no doubt in my mind that if Thomas Jefferson, Abraham Lincoln, or Franklin Roosevelt were seeking office today, they would be unelectable because of some past action. We would find a reason, and some have been discovered through the years, not to elect them. Let me make myself clear. There is a difference in the pattern of repeated behavior throughout one's life and isolated events that may have taken place in one's youth. I can tell you without reservation that I would not be in the ministry if someone paraded my past in front of the church I was called to serve.

Several years ago, our church elected a man to serve as a deacon who was a recovering alcoholic. He had not had a drink in over twenty years. I would say that ninety-nine percent of the church knew his past because he grew up in that community. He told me he didn't think he was worthy to serve. I told him God was more concerned with where an individual was right now, rather than in their past. One mistake doesn't signal divine foreclosure on a life. Too bad it does today in the political world. People in glass houses shouldn't throw stones. I know I'm guilty, but I also know God has forgiven me.

Godspeed my friends.

> *For in the same way you judge others, you will be judged, and with the measure you use, it will be measured to you. Why do you look at the speck of sawdust in your brother's eye and pay no attention to the plank in your own eye?*
> ~Matthew 7:2-3 NIV

START HERE...

Do You Get It?

Over the years I have observed as a pastor that some folks "get it" and others don't. Mr. John most definitely gets it. Over the years, more than seventy if you're counting, life has dealt this sweet man some serious blows. He has known the pain of losing a wife, and he has battled cancer. A few years ago, he spent six weeks in the hospital battling this fierce opponent and finally got back to nearly full speed. He moves a little slower these days, as he walks with a cane, but it hasn't stopped him from serving his God.

One particular Wednesday night, following our time of Bible study, Mr. John came to me with an idea of how he could help our office workers at the church. Each week our order of worship is filled with extra pieces of paper. One of those is the outline of the morning message, while others include sign-up sheets for various trips and other information. He asked if he could come to the church each week and stuff our bulletins. He has faithfully done just that. Each week, on Thursday, he comes to the church with his CD player and sits in a room adjacent to our office and goes to work. While he's working, he's listening and singing those old gospel tunes. Yesterday, I walked into his room. He had his back to me. He did not have a clue that I was watching him and listening to him. A tear rolled down my cheek as I heard him sing:

> *So I'll cherish the old rugged cross,*
> *Till my trophies at last I lay down;*
> *I will cling to the old rugged cross,*
> *And exchange it some day for a crown.*

No person on this earth has ever spoken any truer words. Well done, John; you ministered to me when I needed it most. Thank you for actually getting it. It is a life of service. Do what you can while you can.

Godspeed my friends.

Whoever finds their life will lose it, and whoever loses their life for my sake will find it.
                                ~Matthew 10:39 NIV

START HERE...

You Are of Great Worth

There are certain things I hear from time to time that break my heart as a pastor and as a person. It's when someone shares with me that they have been told they are not good enough. These words, for the most part, have been uttered by a parent, spouse, sibling, teacher, and yes, in some cases, even by a minister. How devastating it is to hear from someone you love and trust that you're worthless and without hope. I have watched and listened to the stories over the years from broken individuals who have lived under that lie for years.

If you've ever felt this way or been told this by another, don't believe it, because it's a devil's lie. You need to understand that you are the crown of God's creation. You are created a little less than the angels. Before creating the earth, God had you on His mind. You are not a mistake; as a matter of fact, you are uniquely and wonderfully made. Your value was proven when Christ died on a cross so that you might have life and have it more abundantly. You matter more than you'll ever know.

Look in the mirror. When you see your reflection, remember this: If you had been the only one on earth, Christ would have died for you. Talk about worth! More than you may ever realize.

Godspeed my friends.

> *What is mankind that you are mindful of them, human beings that you care for them? You have made them a little lower than the angels and crowned them with glory and honor.*
> ~Psalm 8:4-5 NIV

START HERE...

Can You Get Over It?

Getting over the pain experienced in life is easier said than done. It doesn't matter if the wound was inflicted yesterday, last month, or even years ago. "Getting on with it," as so many encourage us to do, is almost impossible because we're not sure how to begin. There is no magical cure for a broken spirit or a shattered heart. So where does one begin?

First and foremost, you need to remember you're not in the battle alone. Scripture reminds us that trouble, grief, and pain are a natural part of life. In the book of Job, the writer reminds us: "Yet man is born to trouble as surely as sparks fly upward" (Job 5:7 NIV). So, if you know it's coming, prepare for the bad times during the good days in life. Also remember, God has promised us that nothing separates us from his love and presence.

Second, you get to decide how long you'll bear the anger and the pain. Now, this isn't necessarily true with grief, but it is true when someone does us wrong. The longer you hold on to the grudge, the more damage it does to your life. The amazing thing is, it does nothing to the person who hurt you. So, pray for that individual as you also pray for yourself. A funny and unusual thing will happen: your bitterness will begin to dissolve. It will strengthen your relationship with God and others.

Finally, realize that life is just too short to go around with a bitter spirit. No one, I mean no one wants to be around a grumpy and complaining individual. That's just a fact. So, it's up to you. How long will you bear the grudge? Relief begins one prayer at a time.

Godspeed my friends.

> *Create in me a pure heart, O God, and renew a steadfast spirit within me.*
>
> ~Psalm 51:10 NIV

START HERE...

Don't Look Back

My brother Richard taught me how to ride a bike. I remember it like it was yesterday. My training ground was the sidewalk just across the street from our home at 1101 College Street in Cleveland, Mississippi. It wasn't the easiest task to accomplish, but we finally got it done. It all came down to a matter of trust. As I recall, he'd run behind me and hold on to the seat of the bike while I peddled with all my might. Then he'd let go, and I'd turn my head and look back at him and then I would fall. In a moment of complete exasperation, he said: "You'll never do this if you keep looking back! Keep peddling and look ahead." It was now or never; we took off. I peddled, and he let go earlier than I expected. I kept my eyes focused on where I was going and rode solo for the first time.

    The problem with so many of us today is, we continue to look back at the past and lose focus on where we are and where we're going. God wants to bless and use you in the present, but we keep focusing on the victories and defeats from the past. As God moves us forward, he keeps telling us: "Keep peddling, keep running, keep moving; because there's so much I want to do through you." But, here is the kicker, unlike my brother Richard, God will never let go. His hand will always be on your shoulder. That is a promise that can move you out of the past and into the present.

    Godspeed my friends.

> *Jesus replied, "No one who puts a hand to the plow and looks back is fit for service in the kingdom of God."*
>
> ~Luke 9:62 NIV

START HERE...

Why Do We Suffer?

I wish I had a dollar for every time I have been asked: "Why is there so much suffering in the world?" The truth of the matter is, there is no simple answer. When you look at the world in which we live, you notice bad things happen to good people every day. Some of the most devout people I have known have had cancer, heart disease, or some other physical problem. Others have suffered through grief, depression, and other emotional setbacks. And yet, if we're all honest with ourselves, in those dark moments of life we ask: "Where was God when these tragedies occurred?"

First, we need a valid concept of God. When we look at the life of Jesus, we can see who God is. In Jesus, we see that God is loving, merciful, and forgiving. He does not send suffering to anyone, but He does allow these things to happen because of the free will he gives to His children. When we violate the laws of His universe, we invite destruction into our lives.

Second, we need a valid concept of the world. Sin is our rebellion against God. But not all evil comes as a result of personal choices. There is a natural evil that exists in our world. When you grasp that, then you can have a better understanding of suffering. When God created the world, he said: "It is good." He didn't say it was perfect.

Finally, God uses pain and suffering to help us grow as Christians. Through trials and tribulations, we develop character and faith. Setbacks become springboards for Christian growth. How do I know this? Read Romans 8:28. If you want to know more about this concept, I'll be preaching on this subject tomorrow. You can find all my sermons on our webpage.

Godspeed my friends.

Not only so, but we also glory in our sufferings, because we know that suffering produces perseverance; perseverance, character; and character, hope. And hope does not put us to shame, because God's love has been poured out into our hearts through the Holy Spirit, who has been given to us.

~Romans 5:3-5 NIV

START HERE...

Keep Discipline Alive

Just recently a school outside Augusta, Georgia (a moment of silence please), made national news because they have decided to bring back paddling as a form of punishment. The parents had to sign a consent form to allow the school officials to carry out this form of discipline on their children. The alternative to paddling was a week of in-school suspension. Around thirty-five percent of the parents signed the form allowing school officials to carry out this action. The story went on to say that this form of discipline is still prevalent in thirteen different states. There's no doubt that this is a subject that we can debate until the cows come home, and yet, change no one's mind or opinion. But there's no doubt in my mind that young people today have little fear and respect for authority. Why? Because they've never been wrong, and Mama and Daddy fight all their battles for them.

If parents disciplined more at home, it would not be a major problem in our schools. I well remember the philosophy in our home as a child; it was simple and understandable. "If you get in trouble at school and get punished, you can expect to be dealt with quickly and severely at home." Also, 99.9 percent of the time, our parents sided with the teachers. We were taught to say, "Yes sir" and "Yes ma'am." As James Dobson has suggested: "Parenting isn't for cowards."

I find it interesting that we can agree that the greatest generation of our nation was the World War II generation. We've abandoned the principles they lived by and embraced. Maybe in a progressive society, we need to look back at some of the qualities from the past that made us the great nation we are today. Discipline is right at the top of the list. A parent who lovingly disciplines their child will gain respect from that child. The parents that do not discipline can expect a lifetime of heartache because they're probably going to experience it. You don't have to abuse a child to discipline them, but you do have to parent them. It's your job. After all, doesn't God discipline his children? Just something to ponder.

Godspeed my friends.

> *Whoever spares the rod hates their children, but the one who loves their children is careful to discipline them.*
>
> ~Proverbs 13:24 NIV

START HERE...

Quitting Is Easy and Takes No Talent

The other day I heard an interesting story about a high school football team in California. After two games the team decided to cancel the remaining games for the year. The reason? They lost the first two games rather decisively and just decided to quit because they weren't very good. The story went on to say that the school officials, the student body, and the community were disappointed by the team's decision. Nevertheless, they canceled the rest of the season.

As I listened to this story, I became infuriated. You see, here's one of the biggest problems in our society. We've developed a mentality that says: "Hey if I don't like something, I'll just quit." Because of this, we're raising a society of quitters. If the piano lessons become too hard, don't worry, you can quit. If the job is too demanding, don't fret, you can quit. If your marriage is too complicated, just quit. And when life becomes too much, yep, you can quit that as well. Whatever happened to the philosophy: "If you start something, finish it."?

I wonder how the lives of these players will turn out? I can tell you this: if one becomes a surgeon, I do not want that one operating on one of my loved ones or me. Most of them will end up living at home with the parents that supported this selfish decision. You reap what you sow. That is something with which they will all have to live.

Paul encouraged young Timothy to finish strong. There is honor in finishing my friend. Oh, don't worry; I'm sure all the players on the team received a nice "participation trophy," ordered and paid for by their parents. Good grief! And we wonder sometimes.

Godspeed my friends.

> *I have fought the good fight, I have finished the race, I have kept the faith.*
>
> ~2 Timothy 4:7 NIV

START HERE...

Ten Easy Steps

Several years ago, while I was pastoring another church, we had a young man who had made his profession of faith during Vacation Bible School. However, for him to fully understand his decision, his parents brought him to my office to discuss his decision and to make sure he understood what he was doing. At the end of our discussion, I told him that he would need to walk the aisle at the end of one of our services during the hymn of invitation. Being a somewhat shy young man, he asked if he could do it on a Tuesday night. When I informed him that we didn't have services on Tuesday night, he said: "I know; I don't want to do this in front anyone."

I understand that there are individuals who have real anxiety when it comes to crowds and getting in front of others. But I also know there are moments when we must conquer our fears. As we talked further, I told this young man about how Jesus walked the streets of Jerusalem with a cross on his back most of the way to Calvary. We then walked down to our sanctuary and sat where he and his family usually sat on Sunday mornings during our service. We got up and counted the steps to the altar. It was less than ten. I asked him if he could take ten steps for Jesus? After a long pause, he assured me he could.

On the following Sunday morning, as our worship service was about to end, we had transitioned into our time of invitation. Immediately this young man came down and took me by the hand before the whole church. I whispered into his ear: "How hard was that walk?" His reply: "The easiest ten steps I ever walked." Sometimes all it takes is just a little perspective on the Christian faith. When we truly understand what Jesus did for us, how can we not follow Him?

Godspeed my friends.

> *Whoever acknowledges me before others, I will also acknowledge before my Father in heaven.*
>
> ~Matthew 10:32 NIV

START HERE...

Reconnecting with the Master

I'm not sure Kane knew what he was getting into when he decided to run with me this morning. He caught up with me around mile two of a five-mile plus run this morning. We didn't say much to each other, and I noticed he was more of an interval runner. That means he'd run for a while and stop, then catch back up with me. He did this for over three miles. When I arrived home, I went inside, prepared a cup of coffee, grabbed my Gatorade, and went outside. I noticed he was still there, trying to catch his breath. I wasn't sure what to do; it was kind of awkward. Wasn't our time together done? I guess not.

I noticed he had a collar around his neck and a little identification bone with his name, address, owner and phone number. I called his owner who lived at least two miles away and informed him that Kane was with me on my front porch. When the white truck pulled into my driveway, Kane's tail began to wag. The man got out, opened the back door of his truck, and Kane jumped inside. The man thanked me and drove off. It was a satisfying sight to see the two back where they belonged. All it took was a little phone call.

If you find yourself drifting away from your Master and it seems as though all is lost, remember, He's just a prayer away. When you call upon His name, He opens the door for you to come home. Just like Kane, you can be back with the one who loves you.

Godspeed my friends.

> *So he got up and went to his father. But while he was still a long way off, his father saw him and was filled with compassion for him; he ran to his son, threw his arms around him and kissed him. The son said to him, "Father, I have sinned against heaven and against you. I am no longer worthy to be called your son." But the father said to his servants, "Quick! Bring the best robe*

and put it on him. Put a ring on his finger and sandals on his feet. ... For this son of mine was dead and is alive again; he was lost and is found." So they began to celebrate.

~Luke 15:20-22, 24 NIV

START HERE...

Lift Your Eyes

I have noticed over the years that a tragedy will do one of two things to individuals. It will either draw them closer to God or move them further from Him. If it moves them further away, the person is working with the mindset that God caused this tragic situation. So often someone will say to me: "Why did God do this to me?" We need to remember what the Psalmist said: "I will lift up my eyes to the mountains—where does my help come from? My help comes from the Lord, the Maker of heaven and earth" (Psalm 121:1-2 NIV). Notice it did not say: "My tragedy comes from the Lord." You see, we live in a fallen world where bad things happen to good people. That is just the reality of life. God doesn't send bad things, but he does allow them based on our free will of choice.

Then, there are those who draw closer to God in moments of heartbreak. They find the strength they never imagined. They may not mount up on eagle's wings, or run, or even walk. But strength is given to stand. Suddenly, when the fog begins to lift, they notice they haven't been standing alone. The hand of God has been on their shoulder the whole time. Draw closer to God in the darkness, and you'll find He's right by your side.

Godspeed my friends.

> *But those who hope in the Lord will renew their strength. They will soar on wings like eagles; they will run and not grow weary, they will walk and not be faint.*
>
> ~Isaiah 40:31 NIV

START HERE...

Is It What It Is?

There's a catchphrase that I seem to hear an awful lot these days. It seems to describe almost every situation in life, whether good or bad. The sentence which is repeated over and over to me in times of deep and even troubling situations is simply this: "It is what it is." These five words have become an excuse to accept the unacceptable. "Mom and I haven't talked since that huge argument we had, but it is what it is." "Our son's behavior has become uncontrollable. Now the school has suspended him. But it is what it is." "My spouse and I rarely communicate anymore, but it is what it is." "Our church seems to be in turmoil all the time, but it is what it is."

This quote has become an excuse to accept bad and even ungodly behavior. It's as if we've thrown up our hands and said: "This situation can't be changed because it is what it is." But maybe we should ask a question which might change the way we view things. "Is it what it has to be?" With a little effort and a lot of prayers, things don't have to be what they are. They can be what God designed them to be. But you can't be lazy in your faith and your relationships with God and others.

It can start today by just changing an attitude of acceptance to an attitude of determination. By yourself, you may not be able to change, but God can change anyone. Then, and only then, "It can be what He wants it to be."

Godspeed my friends.

> *For the flesh desires what is contrary to the Spirit, and the Spirit what is contrary to the flesh. They are in conflict with each other, so that you are not to do whatever you want. But if you are led by the Spirit, you are not under the law. ... But the fruit of the Spirit is love, joy, peace, forbearance, kindness, goodness, faithfulness, gentleness and self-control. Against such things there is no law.*
>
> ~Galatians 5:17-18, 22-23 NIV

START HERE...

Giving Hope to the Hopeless

The tear stains on my shirt hadn't even dried by the time we got back to my car. The visit to the Intensive Care Unit to check on some old friends and to offer a word of encouragement had lasted about thirty minutes. You leave a family who is clinging to hope that their loved one can somehow make a drastic turn and begin the road to recovery. However, it seems as if she takes two steps back every time she takes one step forward. These are the ones that suck the life out of ministers. After all, what would you expect when you baptized Dad, Mom, and both daughters at the same time. As you get in your vehicle, the feeling of helplessness overwhelms you, because there is not one single thing you can do, but pray.

Suddenly it hits you. The Holy Spirit reminds you of the most important fact of all: you represent the One who offers hope. You are the one who prays, but God is the one who does the work. Just as He meets the needs of the hurting and grieving, He comes to his servant and says: "Get up and eat, for the journey is too much for you" (1 Kings 19:7b NIV). My job is not to "be hope," but to offer hope in the name of Christ. But when you see the tear stains on the shirt, it becomes a little more difficult to remember your role. Trust the director, for He not only knows the scene, but He also authored the entire work.

Godspeed my friends.

> *"For I know the plans I have for you," declares the Lord, "plans to prosper you and not to harm you, plans to give you hope and a future."*
>
> ~Jeremiah 29:11 NIV

START HERE...

God is Greater than Your Sins

"If you really knew me, you wouldn't like me at all." I can't tell you how many times someone has sat in my office and uttered those words. "You just don't know what I have done and the things I have said. If you only knew, you'd turn your head in disgust." There are so many individuals out there walking around with a load of guilt and two loads of shame, based on things that happened twenty years ago in their lives. They want to find relief and redemption, but they're not sure it's available to them. These people have somehow convinced themselves that God's grace can cover everyone else's sins but theirs.

Sometimes as individuals we do not need to be reminded of how bad we are, but rather how good God truly is. No matter the sin or the action, Christ died for you. And the amazing thing is if he had to do it again, He would. If you feel as though you've destroyed the bridge that grace crosses over, please remember that you're the crown of God's creation. God created you in His image and for His pleasure. No matter how dark the night is in your life, his light will shine. No matter how grotesque the action, His blood covers it all. Sometimes we need to accept the fact that we are acceptable.

You see it boils down to this simple thought process. Stop thinking about how bad you are and start rejoicing at how good God is. His love and forgiveness are enough for you.

Godspeed my friends.

> *If we claim to be without sin, we deceive ourselves and the truth is not in us. If we confess our sins, he is faithful and just and will forgive us our sins and purify us from all unrighteousness. If we claim we have not sinned, we make him out to be a liar and his word is not in us.*
>
> ~1 John 1:8-10 NIV

START HERE...

Listen to the Right Voice

If you're told something negative long enough, especially by someone you love or trust, it's hard not to believe it, even when it's not true. Let me give you an example. A young girl comes into the house all excited about being chosen to sing in the school choir, only to hear her mother say: "Why did they choose you? You can't sing." It doesn't matter that the girl can sing like an angel; she now is convinced she can't. She sees herself in the same light as the most important person in her life sees her.

I'm convinced today that you hear two voices in your head. No, I'm not suggesting that you're mentally ill, but two voices are vying for your attention. One voice is telling you that your life doesn't matter and that no one cares. That voice continues by saying if people really knew you, they'd turn their back on you. However, there is another voice that's whispering in your ear. It's hard to hear at times because of the noise of the world. That voice is telling you that you are valued and loved. That voice keeps reminding you that you are worth dying for. That voice will tell you over and over that He knows everything about you and loves you still.

When God becomes the most important person in your life, then you start seeing the beauty He sees in you. You'll see yourself in the same light as the most important person in your life sees you. Listen to His voice; He has never been wrong, and He won't be wrong today.

Godspeed my friends.

> *Are not two sparrows sold for a penny? Yet not one of them will fall to the ground outside your Father's care. And even the very hairs of your head are all numbered. So don't be afraid; you are worth more than many sparrows.*
>
> ~Matthew 10:29-31 NIV

START HERE...

The Real King

It's kind of ironic that the King of Rock and Roll and the Queen of Soul died on the same day forty-one years apart. Both Elvis and Aretha brought so much joy and change to the world. Elvis combined soul and country music and produced what we now know as Rock and Roll. His sound was different, and he changed music forever.

Aretha was just different. As a pastor's daughter, she took gospel music and combined it with soul and gave us a sound that shook us to our very core. When you heard "R-E-S-P-E-C-T," you heard Aretha at her very best. That song ranked number two in the all-time list of top one hundred rock and roll songs. "Satisfaction" by the Stones was number one.

As I watched and listened to the tributes to the Queen of Soul last night, so many echoed the same thoughts. So many said: "She'll live on through her music, just like Elvis." So true.

Over two thousand years ago, the King of Kings died on a Roman cross. It is finished. The religious and political leaders sure thought it was. After all, isn't that what He, Himself, cried from the cross? But three days later, everything changed. Through his resurrection, he conquered Death and Hell with one victorious action. He doesn't live through words printed in a book or stories told about Him. Unlike Elvis and Aretha, He is alive and well, and He is still changing lives today. I love the music of Elvis and Aretha, and they both changed the cultural landscape of our world. Jesus not only created the world, but He changed it. And he's still changing lives today for all eternity. That is the King of Kings and Lord of Lords.

Godspeed my friends.

> *That at the name of Jesus every knee should bow, in heaven and on earth and under the earth, and every tongue acknowledge that Jesus Christ is Lord, to the glory of God the Father.*
> ~Philippians 2:10-11 NIV

START HERE...

Grief Waits its Turn

Most of us are familiar with the seven stages of grief, which include shock, denial, anger, bargaining, depression, testing, and, ultimately, acceptance. I can remember in college psychology studying these basic principles and wondering how they affected an individual's life. Over the past few months, I have had an opportunity to minister to a lot of grieving people. So often I'm asked: "When will this hurt go away? At one point I think I'm fine, the next I'm falling apart. What's wrong with me?"

If you have ever felt that way, then you need to understand you are normal. You see there's no one size fits all when it comes to grief. No schedule comes with grief. In other words, you cannot get a calendar and map out the grief process. It is different for different people. But what I will tell you is there is healthy grief and unhealthy grief. There is constructive grief and destructive grief. There is hopeless grief, and there is grief that is comforted by hope.

Grief always waits its turn. You can deny it, push it back, ignore it; but, sooner or later, you must deal with it. Grief is personal. But so is the comfort of God. Be honest with Him in your feelings and allow His presence to move you forward. Find a friend, a minister, or a counselor to talk to about your struggles. There is always strength in numbers. Remember, you do not have to travel this road alone. Help is usually a phone call or a prayer away.

Godspeed my friends.

Blessed are those who mourn, for they will be comforted.
~Matthew 5:4 NIV

START HERE...

Forgiving Yourself

Sometimes the hardest person to forgive is our self. Let me explain. A couple of weeks ago I called a dear friend of mine whose father had died. We talked soon after they had finished visitation at the funeral home. I asked my old friend how he was dealing with everything, and he replied: "Not good." You see, the last few days of his father's life had been difficult. He had had dementia and several other physical ailments. If you've never dealt with an irrational sick senior adult, consider yourself blessed. It's hard emotionally, physically, and spiritually. Sometimes you have to be stern and forceful with them.

Well, my friend told me he was feeling guilty because of some of the things he had said to his Dad. My response to him was simple. "Don't have a higher standard of forgiveness than God." All of a sudden you could feel the tension and burden begin to ease up over the phone. Choking back the tears, my friend said: "I needed to hear that! You'll never know how much this call has meant to me."

Sometimes it's easy to forgive others, but we fail to let ourselves off the hook. Don't have a higher standard of forgiveness than God when it comes to forgiving yourself.

Godspeed my friends.

For I will forgive their wickedness and will remember their sins no more.

~Hebrews 8:12 NIV

START HERE...

The Table is Prepared for You

The other night, while we were eating in a restaurant just outside of Nashville, I saw a middle-aged couple come in and take a seat just a few tables across from us. They were behind Tommi Jo. She could not see them, but there was no reason to call them to her attention. I noticed something interesting about the man. For some reason, he was a bit unsettled. He got up about three times and then would sit down in a different position. It was as if he were anxious or nervous about something. Occasionally my eyes would be drawn back to this couple.

About ten minutes after their arrival, a young man with fairly long hair entered the restaurant. More than likely he was a college student or a young professional. He looked around the room as if he were trying to find someone. When he spotted this couple, he made his way toward them. When the man saw him coming in his direction, he immediately got up and quickly walked his way. When the two met, the older man threw his arms around the younger one, and they embraced. A million scenarios went through my mind as to what was going on. Could this be a father and mother meeting their college son for dinner? Maybe it was a strained relationship. Maybe this was the first step in restoration. Who knows? But it was beautiful.

This scene took me back to my college years. Every so often my Dad would have to travel to Jackson for a meeting or convention. He'd always call me up at school and set up a dinner meeting. When we met, he always greeted me with a hug and a kiss. Such memories are priceless and irreplaceable. I miss those days.

Similarly, the Heavenly Father is waiting for some of us to come back to Him. He has prepared a table for you. He is patiently waiting. What you'll find when you decide to meet Him is that he runs to you and throws his arms around you. No matter where you've been or what you've done, He's ready to meet you. That is one appointment you don't want to miss.

Godspeed my friends.

You prepare a table before me in the presence of my enemies.
You anoint my head with oil; my cup overflows.
$\qquad\qquad\qquad\qquad\qquad\qquad$ ~Psalm 23:5 NIV

START HERE...

Fight the Good Fight

While on the campus of The Southern Baptist Theological Seminary in Louisville, Kentucky, my alma mater, I noticed the new students were registering and getting ready for the fall semester. I wanted to ask them if they really knew what they were signing up for in life. After more than thirty years in the ministry, I wanted to pull a couple of them to the side and give them a little information.

For example, do they understand that only forty percent of those who graduate will ever serve a local church? That was the statistic when I finished, and it could be higher or lower. Do they understand that about eighty percent of the things they will deal with will be negative? Things like death, marriage counseling, cancer, heart disease, and the loss of friends. Do they understand the 80-10-10 rule in the local church? Eighty percent will like them if they do a good job. Ten percent will think they are the greatest thing since sliced bread. And ten percent will hate them regardless of what they do.

I wonder if they know what it feels like to have people you trust betray you? It happened to Jesus, so don't expect it to be any different for the minister. Will they understand the grind of being on call twenty-four/seven, while most folks think you only work two days a week? Will they expect people to get jealous when they make friends within the church? Will they be ready for an occasional anonymous letter? Will they understand the loneliness that comes with the job? Will they expect the heartbreak of burying a friend? Do they realize that churches fire ministers at a rate of two hundred a month? Do they comprehend that when you leave a church, you leave all your friends behind? Do they know there will be moments when they question their call to ministry? And yes, at times, they may even question God Himself.

On the other hand, do they know the thrill they'll experience when they lead someone to Christ? Are they aware that they'll see lives transformed right before their eyes? Do they know that their faith will be tested, but as a result of the testing, it will grow stronger? Do they know that calls will come years later from people who will say: "You made a difference."?

I wanted to tell one or two that it's going to be hard, but in the end, it will be worth it. So, "fight the good fight, finish the race, and keep the faith."

Godspeed my friends.

> *Fight the good fight of the faith. Take hold of the eternal life to which you were called when you made your good confession in the presence of many witnesses.*
> ~1 Timothy 6:12 NIV

START HERE...

Leave it on the Road

Back in 2009, I got this bright idea to run in my first marathon. Yep, 26.2 miles of running delight. For months I trained as hard as I had ever trained before. In other words, by the time race day was here, my body, my mind, and my spirit were ready. If you've never run a marathon, one thing you need to know is that most runners view the race as two separate runs – the first 20 miles and the last 6.2 miles. Around mile twenty-two, I was struggling. To give my body a rest, I walked for about a quarter of a mile. However, as I approached the finish line, I saw my younger daughter, Melanie, holding up a sign which read: "Leave it on the road, Daddy!!" It was just the shot of adrenaline I needed. Suddenly the pain took a back seat and a surge of energy shot through my body. All it took was a word of encouragement.

The same is true in this race we call life. There are some of us who are hurting, suffering, and struggling to get through. We are trying to push through the pain and the darkness but quitting seems much easier and desirable. Maybe what we need is a little encouragement. Maybe we need to be reassured of someone's love and support. Quite possibly, we need to remember we are not alone.

One valuable lesson I've learned over the years of my running is: I have to focus on where I'm going and not look back at where I've been. The same is true in our lives. Stop thinking about the failures of the past and focus on the task of the present. You can do this! How do I know? Because you are not alone. There's a power of a presence available to you this day. When the race gets too long and the hills too steep, walk. Don't stop. Keep moving. In other words, leave it on the road! Finish strong. You and the Lord have this. I have faith in you. Encourage others as you run your race. Even in your struggles, you can be a difference-maker.

Godspeed my friends.

For I am already being poured out like a drink offering, and the time for my departure is near. I have fought the good fight, I have finished the race, I have kept the faith.
~2 Timothy 4:6-7 NIV

START HERE...

Be Sure to Hold Hands

When I was a child, and we traveled to Memphis, Tennessee, or Jackson, Mississippi, we often parked in a nearby garage and walked to our destination. When we would come to a busy intersection, my dad would extend his hand to me, and I would immediately hold it while we crossed the street. Holding hands with my dad was a common practice of my childhood.

When I was sixteen, my Dad and I were in Memphis once again. We found ourselves at one of those busy streets, and when the time came to cross, Dad floated his hand towards mine. I looked at him and said: "I think I've got this one." I'll never forget the look on his face. He wasn't trying to embarrass me or make me feel inferior. He was looking out for his son. He realized at that moment that I didn't need his assistance. It's a moment every parent faces sooner or later. There are times when we need to hold on as mothers and dads, and there are times we need to let go.

However, over the last thirteen years, I've missed those hands. There have been moments when I've needed a little assistance or guidance in my own life. But in those times when I struggle, there's another hand that reaches towards me and a small voice that says: "I'm here! Don't be afraid." It's the same hand that pulled Peter out of the water. It's the same hand that touched the blind, the lame, and the deaf. It's the same hand that is offered to you when you face an onslaught of traffic at a dangerous intersection in life. Let that hand not only comfort you but also guide you to safety. It's the hand of your Heavenly Father. The good news about that hand is that it will never leave nor forsake you.

Godspeed my friends.

"Come," he said. Then Peter got down out of the boat, walked on the water and came toward Jesus. But when he saw the

wind, he was afraid and, beginning to sink, cried out, "Lord, save me!" Immediately Jesus reached out his hand and caught him. "You of little faith," he said, "why did you doubt?"

~Matthew 14:29-31 NIV

START HERE...

The Only Difference is Knowledge

You've completed all the necessary tests the doctor has ordered, and now you wait anxiously for the results. The minutes seem more like hours, and finally, the physician walks in with your folder and results. He looks at you and says those three words no one wants to hear: "You have cancer." At that point, your whole life changes, or so it seems. However, the only difference between that moment and the day before is "knowledge." The cancer was in your body before the appointment, but you were not aware of its presence. Now you know.

The scene changes. Mom and Dad are in the den. Picture an average everyday family. They have done their best to raise their children in a Christian environment. Their oldest daughter comes in and informs her parents that she is pregnant. At that moment, everything seems to change for that family. At that moment all of their hopes and dreams are shattered. However, the only difference between that moment and the day before is "knowledge." Now they know.

You have a friend, and unbeknownst to you, she has been spreading lies about you or your family. However, one day the lie gets back to you. You discover what she has been saying to others regarding your reputation. The only difference between the day you find out and the day before is "knowledge." Now you know.

Knowledge is a powerful tool in one's life. What you do with that knowledge says everything about your character, faith, morals, and ethics. Two wrongs have never made a right. God expects you to rise above the circumstances of life and be a living testimony to Him. He will walk with you regardless of the situation and never forsake you. So now that you know, what are you going to do with the knowledge? Choose wisely.

Godspeed my friends.

That night God appeared to Solomon and said to him, "Ask for whatever you want me to give you." Solomon answered God, "You have shown great kindness to David my father and have made me king in his place. Now, Lord God, let your promise to my father David be confirmed, for you have made me king over a people who are as numerous as the dust of the earth. Give me wisdom and knowledge, that I may lead this people, for who is able to govern this great people of yours?"

~2 Chronicles 1:7-10 NIV

START HERE...

Love Conquers All

When I see what is happening in the state of New York and their recent law on abortion, the Holy Spirit reminds me of the following passage of scripture: "In those days there was no king in Israel: every man did that which was right in his own eyes" (Judges 21:25 KJV). Do you see the major emphasis in that sentence? There is a huge difference in doing what is right in one's own eyes and doing what is right in God's eyes. Jiminy Cricket said: "Let your conscience be your guide." The problem with that mentality is, some folks have little or no conscious at all. Maybe, just maybe, we need to allow the Spirit of God to be our guide. That would be a novel approach.

However, let me give you a word of caution. "And now these three remain: faith, hope and love. But the greatest of these is love" (1Corinthians 13:13 NIV). Always speak the truth in love. Do not back down, but whatever you say, print, post, or write, do so in love. The world will know we are followers of Christ by our love, not by what we boycott or hate, but by our love. Pray for the spirit of God to pour out on those who need it. There is already enough hate in our world to destroy it ten times over. Yes, this entire situation is sickening to me and my beliefs. I will stand and at the top of my lungs be a Pro-life advocate. But my Lord commands me to love my neighbor and pray for those who persecute me. Believe me; the left will persecute those who do not agree with them. As a matter of fact, those who preach tolerance are the least tolerant people on the planet.

Lord Jesus, we need you now more than ever.

Godspeed my friends.

> *Instead, speaking the truth in love, we will grow to become in every respect the mature body of him who is the head, that is, Christ.*
>
> ~Ephesians 4:15 NIV

START HERE...

Finding Light in the Midst of Darkness

Last night I came upon a most interesting and, at first glance, a rather annoying sight – three cars in a row traveling about twenty miles per hour. It didn't take long to figure out the situation. The middle car had no lights. The car in the front was leading with its lights. The car in the rear had its flashers on to signal caution to the traffic behind. In other words, those two were helping the one in the dark.

There are times in our life when the light of Christ either grows dim or shuts off altogether. Due to the circumstances and, sometimes, the onslaught of life, we find ourselves in the dark and feeling alone. Before you know it, out of nowhere, a light appears. It may come from a note, a text, a hug, a word of encouragement or even a friendly visit. These are little God winks that the Lord sends our way to remind us we're not alone. I can't tell you how many times in my life I've felt alone and isolated. In those solitude moments, I've questioned my calling and my faith. The light may not be out, but there's an eclipse at midday. Suddenly, a small light shines through an unexpected source. And when I say unexpected, I mean so unexpected it could come from no one else but God. Does it make a difference? You bet it does.

Remember, John, in his writings, reminded us: "And the light shineth in darkness; and the darkness comprehended it not" (John 1:5 KJV). You are never left alone in the darkness because there is always the One who knows how to turn on the light. Just fall in behind Him, and He will guide you home.

Godspeed my friends.

> *The light shines in the darkness, and the darkness has not overcome it.*
>
> ~John 1:5 NIV

START HERE...

Facing Death with Hope

I've often been asked the question: "How hard is it to do a funeral for someone you don't know?" The answer is always the same: "Not very hard when you have adequate information on the individual." The hard services are for the ones you're the closest to in life. The closer I am to the deceased, the more I must distance myself from the family before the service. In my mind, I must compartmentalize those relationships so that I can do what the family has asked me to do. It is emotionally, physically, mentally, and spiritually exhausting. The older I get, the longer it takes to recuperate.

At every graveside service I do, I tell the grieving family: "I've never sat where you're sitting today. I'm always the one standing by the casket." It was true with my father-in-law, my dad, and my mother. However, God has strengthened me over the years to get through some tough services. My preaching professor in seminary told us: "As the minister, you are the symbol and the personification of hope and strength. If you break down and come apart, it will affect the grieving family." My time to grieve comes later. Sometimes in the still solitude of the night. When you grasp the magnitude of the moment, I have also learned that I must be prayed up and prepared spiritually before the service.

When you lose a loved one, the sting of death is devastating. As a pastor, you feel that sting far too often and it can certainly take its toll. In reality, there is no place I would rather be in that moment, than standing by the casket because of the hope found and realized in Christ Jesus. It is my highest honor as a minister of the gospel.

Godspeed my friends.

Jesus said to her, "I am the resurrection and the life. The one who believes in me will live, even though they die; and whoever lives by believing in me will never die. Do you believe this?"
~John 11:25-26 NIV

START HERE...

Never Alone

We are the proud owners of two miniature schnauzers, Jeter and Lulu. As empty nesters, I guess you could say they're our babies. Why do I say this? Because without a doubt they are spoiled and don't realize they're dogs. That's not always a bad thing. When we travel, they travel with us. They have this unusual ability to know when we're going out of town. All we must do is start packing. They start panicking. It doesn't matter how many times I tell them: "You're going with us." They are a nervous wreck until they get into the car.

However, there are times when they can't travel with us. In that case, we either have to board them or have someone take care of them in our absence. When we come home, they go crazy. I've often wondered what goes through their minds. Are they thinking: "Where are they? Why did they leave? Are they ever coming back? We're so lonely." Thoughts that make me sad.

In a similar sense, I think, as children of God, we suffer the same anxiety. There are moments when we feel as though God has deserted us in our time of need. We feel cold, afraid, lonely, uncertain, and abandoned. But remember this: no matter the circumstances of life, God never leaves us. In the darkness, we may have a difficult time finding him, but his presence is all around us. And just for another point of reference, even though we have the presence of the Holy Spirit, Jesus Himself is coming back! Of this, I am sure.

So, remember, God has not left you as an orphan with no hope and no one to care. If you are feeling alone, draw close to Him. His presence will give you peace.

Godspeed my friends.

Yet I am always with you; you hold me by my right hand.
~Psalm 73:23 NIV

START HERE...

Does God Put More on Us?

I wish I had a dollar for every time I've heard someone say: "You know, God never puts more on you than you can handle." When someone makes this statement, I will ask the individual: "Where did you hear or read that?" Without hesitation, most will say they heard it from a preacher. Some say they read it in the Bible. If they tell me it's in the Bible, then the next question I ask is: "Where?" You see this is a statement we often use to comfort hurting people we love. However, I'm not sure we are very accurate with our assessment of the scriptures.

This statement that God never puts more on us than we can handle is often confused with the following passage of scripture: "No temptation has overtaken you except what is common to mankind. And God is faithful; he will not let you be tempted beyond what you can bear. When you are tempted, he will also provide a way out so that you can endure it" (1 Corinthians 10:13 NIV). Do you see the difference? Because it's huge my friend.

If God didn't allow things to come into our lives which we couldn't handle, why would we need Him? You see, our strength is small and limited. However, there is a supernatural power, a divine power which is available to the children of God. Paul said it best when he said: "I can do all this through him who gives me strength" (Philippians 4:13 NIV). The things I can't handle, God can.

God has not promised us a life free from heartache and pain, but rather God has promised that He will never leave us. Because of that, His strength, love, and presence will guide me through the things I can't handle. As His child, I can live with that. Hopefully, you can too.

Godspeed my friends.

No temptation has overtaken you except what is common to mankind. And God is faithful; he will not let you be tempted beyond what you can bear. But when you are tempted, he will also provide a way out so that you can endure it.

~1 Corinthians 10:13 NIV

START HERE...

Preparation for the Attack

It never fails. Whenever I get a new pair of shoes, someone is going to step on top of them leaving a nice scuff. The same is true with a new necktie; it becomes a magnet for food and coffee. And, heaven forbid, you ever get a new car. Either someone is going to open their door on your new ride, leaving a nice little crease, or a wayward rock is going to find your windshield. These isolated events never happen to your old shoes, ties, or cars. It usually happens to the brand-new item that brings you so much joy.

The same is true with the Christian faith. The moment you start getting excited about your walk with Christ, watch out. Someone's going to step on your spiritual toes or do something that stains your faith. Better yet, the rocks will fly from all directions when you least expect them. You get to the point in life when you think: "I thought once my spiritual life was in step, everything else would fall into place." Don't bank on it, my friend. The attacks from the evil one will come quickly and often to those who are growing in their faith. Why? Satan is not worried about a lukewarm Christian just drifting through life. That kind of believer is Satan's best weapon. However, the moment you start growing in your faith, he will do any and everything he can to trip you and cause you to fall.

Remember, it is a spiritual battle every day. That's why it's important to put on the full armor of God. Unguarded strength is a double weakness in the spiritual walk. Why do you think so many churches are in decline? Why are so many spiritual leaders falling? Be ready. You never know when the battle will come knocking on your front door. May you and I be strong enough today to strike a blow against the forces of evil.

Godspeed my friends.

Put on the full armor of God, so that you can take your stand against the devil's schemes. For our struggle is not against flesh and blood, but against the rulers, against the authorities, against the powers of this dark world and against the spiritual forces of evil in the heavenly realms. Therefore put on the full armor of God, so that when the day of evil comes, you may be able to stand your ground, and after you have done everything, to stand. Stand firm then, with the belt of truth buckled around your waist, with the breastplate of righteousness in place, and with your feet fitted with the readiness that comes from the gospel of peace. In addition to all this, take up the shield of faith, with which you can extinguish all the flaming arrows of the evil one. Take the helmet of salvation and the sword of the Spirit, which is the word of God.

~Ephesians 6:11-17 NIV

START HERE...

Home is Just a Prayer Away

My older daughter came home last night for a quick visit. There are some things she needs before school gets started, so she popped in last night and will leave this afternoon. I don't care what her reasons are for coming home; I just love it when she does. The older I get, the more I cherish just the brief moments I get to spend with my girls. With such a fast-paced world in which we live, sometimes the simple, most important things go unattended. Celebrate the times your family gets together while you still can.

I know God loves it when His children come back to Him. Especially after it's been a long time since He has seen or heard from them. Certain things happen in our lives that drive us into His presence. It could be health related, the death of a loved one, financial difficulties or family struggles. Those trials and setbacks can often be the very thing that God uses to bring you back to Him. Whatever the reason, regardless of the situation, God loves to welcome his children back into His presence. Why don't you call upon His name today? He is ready to help you. Remember, He loves you.

Godspeed my friends.

> *My Father's house has many rooms; if that were not so, would I have told you that I am going there to prepare a place for you? And if I go and prepare a place for you, I will come back and take you to be with me that you also may be where I am.*
> ~John 14:2-3 NIV

START HERE...

The Difference is Commitment

A relationship is always two-sided. The more you invest in another, the more you get. Likewise, the less you give, the less you will receive. That is true in every relationship. You've heard the old expression: "Marriage is 50 – 50." But it's not; it is 100 – 100. If you are only giving fifty percent effort to your relationship with your spouse, you are in trouble. It takes a total commitment from both spouses for that union to blossom and become what God wants it to be.

Likewise, our relationship with God requires a total commitment from us. Do not worry about God holding up His end of the bargain. Remember, at Calvary God demonstrated His commitment to you. But here is where we get confused. Too many people want the blessings of God without putting forth any effort of their own. It is as if we think God owes us something. Nothing could be further from the truth. God doesn't owe us a thing. However, we owe Him everything.

I sometimes have people ask me: "Why isn't God blessing me in my life?" My question back is: "Why should he? What are you doing for him?" Get involved in a personal relationship with your creator. Spend time with Him and get to know Him. You will be surprised at how much better your life will be. The blessings will take care of themselves.

Godspeed my friends.

> *Whatever you do, work at it with all your heart, as working for the Lord, not for human masters.*
> ~Colossians 3:23 NIV

START HERE...

Pain Management

There are some pains and hurts we experience which are so devastating that if we lived two lifetimes, we would never get over them. In reality, there's no expiration date on certain catastrophes in life. Rather than getting over the pain, we must learn to live with and manage the pain. I know this is true in my own life. From time to time certain images march across my mind that causes a sting or prick to my heart. It's not that we dwell on such past events, but certain circumstances bring them back to life. So how do we move away from the hurt and pain?

Some people will say: "You have to forgive and forget." Well, let me set the record straight right at the start. Forgiving and forgetting is impossible. I think a better solution is to forgive, which God demands, and get on with it. You have the choice, as hard as it is, to decide how long you will allow people from your past to continue to hurt you. Once you forgive them, then move on. In other words, don't dwell on it. As soon as someone or something reminds you of the past, remember it is in the past. It is time to move on.

Second, remember that grief is a process and not a moment. The loss of a child, spouse, parent, or friend is something we never really get over. We have to learn to manage the pain. With any physical injury, I've learned to manage the pain. I don't stop moving. I just move differently. One of the best things we can do when grief starts overwhelming us is to do something for someone else. When we help others, it takes the spotlight off of us. Just remember, grief always waits its turn.

Finally, understand there is a power beyond our own that is available to us. Grief and pain are personal, but so is the comfort of God. Draw near to Him. You will be surprised at how close He is, even when He is silent. Darkness can never master His light; what a comforting thought.

Godspeed my friends.

I consider that our present sufferings are not worth comparing with the glory that will be revealed in us.

~Romans 8:18 NIV

START HERE...

The Church May Need to be Like My Gym

I wish the church could be a little more like my gym. Let me explain. Over the last six months or so, I've had to stop working out at my local gym. The doctor diagnosed me with a slap tear in my left shoulder. Instead of surgery, we decided to rest and rehab my shoulder. I've still been able to run in the mornings, but my gym visits have been few and far between. However, yesterday I decided to get back into my routine slowly. I was not quite ready for the reception I received.

When I walked into the facility, one of the workers met me at the door. The first thing out of his mouth was: "The mayor has returned!" Several people came and welcomed me back. Each one of them wanted to know how the shoulder was doing, but also everyone greeted me enthusiastically. One senior adult, Mr. Clete, hugged me so long that I thought he was going to crush me. Then, like my Dad used to do, he kissed me on my cheek and said: "I missed you so much." I must say, it was a bit humbling and encouraging. I'm not great friends with any of these people, but you would think we were fraternity brothers. No one laid a guilt trip on me because of my absence; they were just glad I was there.

When I got in my car to leave, I thought: "This is how the church should be." Too often when wayward souls come back into the fold, we heap guilt on them due to their recent absence. Instead, we ought to rejoice and welcome them back. There are a lot of things we can learn from this experience and use in our churches. People don't need to be reminded about how bad they are, but rather how good God is and how receptive his people can be. Maybe, just maybe, we need to be a little more like the people at the gym.

Godspeed my friends.

Then the master told his servant, "Go out to the roads and country lanes and compel them to come in, so that my house will be full. I tell you, not one of those who were invited will get a taste of my banquet."

~Luke 14:23-24 NIV

START HERE...

Keep It Real at Home and at Church

I've often said one of the biggest forms of hypocrisy is cleaning your house for company. It's as if you're saying: "Yep, we live like this all the time." It's especially hypocritical when the ones visiting are your children. After all, they know exactly how you live and how often you clean the house.

A clean house for guests isn't the only form of hypocrisy these days. Social media has become an outlet for some to communicate to the world that they're living a dream. When in reality they're lost in a nightmare. Forums such as Facebook, Instagram, Twitter, and Snapchat allow individuals to share how good life is for them. Or better yet, it allows them to give the appearance that life is perfect. Remember, anyone can look good online. But sooner or later, one has to face reality. We cannot live our life on social media, but rather, we must live life in the home. "Unless the Lord builds the house, the builders labor in vain" (Psalm 127:1a NIV).

Sad, but true, the church has become a place where we pretend that life is grand. It gives us one more opportunity for hypocrisy. After all, we'd never want anyone to know that our lives are falling apart at the seams. However, we need to remember that the church is for the broken and the hurting. It's refreshing to hear individuals who are honest about their struggles in life. It reminds us that we're not alone in our darkness and fears. Life becomes a little easier when we don't play games, and we come clean with our struggles in life. Very few people have it all together. The rest of us struggle each day to keep our heads above water. If life seems hard and unfair, you're in the majority and not the minority. Just be honest with your feelings before God. He can handle the truth. Remember, He already knows how you feel.

Aren't you tired of pretending you have it all together? "Cast all your anxiety on him because he cares for you" (1 Peter 5:7 NIV). His opinion about you is the only one that matters.

Godspeed my friends.

> *But if serving the Lord seems undesirable to you, then choose for yourselves this day whom you will serve, whether the gods your ancestors served beyond the Euphrates, or the gods of the Amorites, in whose land you are living. But as for me and my household, we will serve the Lord.*
>
> ~Joshua 24:15 NIV

START HERE...

Remember to Say "Thank You"

A simple "thank you" goes a long way. Yesterday while running a few errands, my journey took me to the donut shop to place our church order for Sunday morning. As I was leaving, a young teenage girl was walking in, so I held the door open for her. She walked in and never acknowledged my presence. As she walked by, I said: "You are welcome." Of course, there was no reply from her because of the earphones in her ears. As I walked to my car, I thought: "How rude. She never even thanked me."

As I got in my car, it suddenly hit me. How many times do I say thank you? Do those words roll off my tongue to my family, friends, co-workers, or to the people who show compassion to me? A better question is: "Do I express my gratitude to my Creator, or do I think I'm entitled to the blessings I receive each day?" When we fail to offer a word of thanks, it shows God and others how thoughtless we really are. Don't you remember the story of the ten lepers Jesus healed? Out of ten, only one came back and said thank you. I guess the other nine had their earphones in their ears.

Don't be one of the nine. Take time to say thank you. It does make a difference. Thank you for reading this.

Godspeed my friends.

> *Give thanks in all circumstances; for this is God's will for you in Christ Jesus.*
>
> ~1 Thessalonians 5:18 NIV

START HERE...

Let the Church be the Church

As churches, we do a pretty good job of evangelizing our local battlegrounds. For the most part, we do a good job sending mission groups to foreign and domestic areas. The local church does a great job of leading in Bible studies and worship. However, in my opinion, we do a sorry job in restoration. When it comes to restoring individuals when they've hit a moral bump in the road, we still have a long way to go. Sometimes instead of ministering to the broken, we pronounce judgment upon them and wash our hands of any involvement with them. At the top of the list and leading the way in this endeavor is pastors. It's sad but true.

Last week I was talking to a minister who was going through a tough time. The situation, over which he had no control, had left him without a job and his family in turmoil. In my conversation with him, he said: "The least amount of compassion offered to me has come from my minister friends." I'm sorry, but I thought God had given believers the ministry of reconciliation. The world will tell you: "You made your bed, now lie in it." However, Jesus said: "Take up your bed and walk." Sometimes all a person needs is a little compassion and understanding. You don't have to approve of the situation, but you can help restore the hurting.

Rather than sitting in judgment of the fallen, we need to sit with them and assure them they're not alone. When we do this, we demonstrate the love of Christ. After all, isn't that what we've been called to do?

Godspeed my friends.

> *Brothers and sisters, if someone is caught in a sin, you who live by the Spirit should restore that person gently. But watch yourselves, or you also may be tempted.*
> ~Galatians 6:1 NIV

START HERE...

The Example of Kindness

You would have thought he was running for public office. He spoke to everyone who came in the barbershop. Not only did he speak to everyone, but he also wanted to know everybody's name. The lady cutting his hair had a hard time keeping John Michael's head still. He wanted to know everything about everyone in the building. He was getting his haircut because he was going to see one of his five, yes five, girlfriends. He was not boasting. He was stating a fact. When he finally finished getting all groomed up, he shook hands with everyone sitting down. When he left, we all felt a little better about ourselves and the world. You see, John Michael is fifteen years old, and he has Down syndrome. Over the years of my life, I've come to learn that the closest thing to unconditional love is an individual with Down syndrome.

There's a lot we can learn from John Michael as we journey through life. Just the simple act of being kind to others, regardless of who they are, can make a huge difference. Sometimes a smile, a handshake, an embrace, or a kind word can lift the spirits of another. You might be skeptical about that, but when he left the shop, we were all smiling. Here's an individual who is special needs meeting the needs of other people by just being kind. In reality, our world needs a little more kindness and love.

Thanks, John Michael, for brightening up my day and making me smile. Lord knows I needed it. You, my friend, are indeed special.

Godspeed my friends.

> *Therefore, as God's chosen people, holy and dearly loved, clothe yourselves with compassion, kindness, humility, gentleness and patience.*
> ~Colossians 3:12 NIV

START HERE...

Time to Cut the Apron Strings

Okay, parents, I have a question for you. When are you going to let your children grow up? I'm not talking about your middle school children or even your high school kids. At this point, I'm even going to give your college students a pass. (However, by this time they should be well on their way to adulthood.) I'm referring to your adult children who have children. When are you going to allow them to grow up and accept responsibility for their own lives? When are you going to let them learn lessons based on the mistakes they make? How many times are you going to bail them out of trouble and allow them to believe it's someone else's fault? I can't tell you how many parents are being ruined financially, emotionally, physically, and spiritually because they are not only trying to keep their heads above water, but they're also coming to the rescue of their adult children at every turn. And the reality is this: your children are killing you.

We need to realize a couple of important facts about adulthood. If your child is old enough to get married, then they ought to be old enough to be an adult and accept the responsibilities that go with it. If your child is old enough to have children, then they're old enough to be an adult and accept the responsibilities that go with it. Now understand this: I'm not suggesting that you never help your adult children financially or emotionally. What I am saying is sooner or later they have to understand the world does not owe them a living. When they make mistakes, they need to accept responsibility and learn from them. It is an adult world. We have no choice but to learn to live in it.

Also, you need to understand that if you continue to enable your adult children, it will hurt other relationships. It could damage your relationship with your spouse. It may adversely affect your relationship with your other children. Sometimes we do not realize these negative aspects of our actions until it's too late.

A good parent will love, support and nurture their children. They will also be able to allow their children to grow up. Maybe it's time to cut the cord with your 45-year-old child and let them experience the real world. Both of you will be healthier in the long run.

Godspeed my friends.

> *Start children off on the way they should go, and even when they are old they will not turn from it.*
> ~Proverbs 22:6 NIV

START HERE...

Respect – It's Not a Dirty Word

I do not care if the President invites you to the White House and you choose not to go. That is your business and your decision. I don't care if you disagree with the current President of the United States. That's why we live in the land of the free and the home of the brave. But I do care when athletes and celebrities use profanities and dishonor a position of authority. When one does that in a public forum, it signifies to all that anything goes, and anyone can say or do as they please. When you constantly tear down others, you fail to build up anyone.

When our former president was in office, I disagreed with ninety-nine percent of his policies; however, he was my President. I prayed for him and wanted him to be successful. When he was successful, it was good for the country and good for me. While he was in office, I prayed diligently for him and the decisions he made. The same is true with our current President. However, the thing that makes me the maddest is those who scream tolerance to the top of their lungs are the most intolerant people on the planet. Their idea of tolerance is that one must agree with their point of view.

Nowhere in the Bible does it say we are to hate our leaders. To the contrary, in First Timothy 2:2, we are told to pray for those in authority over us. What would happen at an awards show, if a celebrity took the microphone and said: "Before I present this award, let's pray for our country and our president." That will never happen. But we'll spit out venomous poison to the top of our lungs and get a standing ovation. And we wonder why we're in the shape we're in today. We're spoiled brats, plain and simple. May God help us.

Godspeed my friends.

I urge, then, first of all, that petitions, prayers, intercession and thanksgiving be made for all people – for kings and all those in authority, that we may live peaceful and quiet lives in all godliness and holiness.

~1 Timothy 2:1-2 NIV

START HERE...

The Call is One of Obedience

Last week during Vacation Bible School I had a child ask me: "If you weren't a preacher, what would you be?" That's an interesting question and one that I haven't pondered too often. The simple answer for me would be: "I'd be out of the will of God." You see, I didn't choose this vocation, it chose me. Many years ago, as I was struggling with the call to go into the ministry, my Dad said to me: "If you can be happy doing anything else, do it. However, if God calls you, you will not be happy doing something else." He was always the great simplifier. A pastor or minister is just like anyone else. What sets them apart from others is the call of God for their life.

Today it's harder being a minister than at any other time in history. Part of that is due to the change in society and culture; the other is the high demands of a minister today. Whether we like it or not, numbers often determine the success of a church. If attendance and giving are up, then obviously the church is growing. Members often ask me if I think the church is doing well. To be honest, it is a hard question to answer, because I think God's definition of success is much different than ours. The corporate mindset has become commonplace in our churches. Congregations demand instant results much like a college sports program. The pressure to succeed is, at times, hard to manage even in a minister's life.

All I know is this: God has called me to be obedient rather than successful. If I'm obedient to the call laid on my life, the numbers will take care of themselves. As for the first question about what I'd do if not preaching? The circus is always in need of a few clowns. Pray for your ministers. They need it.

Godspeed my friends.

Do your best to present yourself to God as one approved, a worker who does not need to be ashamed and who correctly handles the word of truth.

~2 Timothy 2:15 NIV

START HERE...

Always Leave the Light On

If you are a parent, it's not a matter of if, but when your child breaks your heart. I don't care how good your baby boy or girl is, sooner or later they will rock you to your very soul. The amount of damage you suffer is directly related to the actions of the child. Also, one needs to understand there are different types of heartbreaks suffered by parents. There's a huge difference between a child rebelling against you as a parent and everything you stand for, and a child exercising their independence as they transition into adulthood. Both can leave a parent in a state of grief and brokenness. However, one is healthy and natural while the other is devastating.

Even though your child can cause you to run down an empty ally and cry "fish," we need to understand an important fact: you can never disown your child for doing wrong. You might want to, but that is not a biblical option. Parents, sometimes you must love your child through the pain, brokenness, and heartbreak. No matter where your child travels, he is still your child.

When I was in college, I would often travel home at night. My mom and dad always left a light on in our den. That light was always a symbol to me that I was welcomed and wanted. Sometimes all you can do as a parent is leave the light on for your child and remind him that he is always welcome at your house. After all, the Father has left His light on for you and me through His Son. Shouldn't we do the same?

Godspeed my friends.

> *For you were once darkness, but now you are light in the Lord. Live as children of light (for the fruit of the light consists in all goodness, righteousness and truth).*
>
> ~Ephesians 5:8-9 NIV

START HERE...

The Ultimate Healing

Many of us know what it's like to sit by the bedside of our loved one and watch them struggle to hang on to life. There's nothing more gut-wrenching than seeing someone you love in a helpless state knowing that the doctors and nurses have done all they can do. As a pastor, I've prayed for healing with these people and their families only to see them pass from this earthly scene. A question comes to me from time to time from the loved ones left behind. "Why didn't God do something? Did he not hear or care about the prayers we prayed?" It is not easy to answer such questions during those times of grief and sorrow.

I can't speak to that which I don't know. However, I can address the questions asked with what I do know and understand. First, I fully believe that God answers every prayer we pray. He answers those prayers according to His will and not ours. Sometimes He answers those petitions with a "yes," while other times He answers with a "no." There are other moments when He says: "Not now." You see, we do not see everything that God sees. In the 13th chapter of First Corinthians, Paul reminds us: "For now we see only a reflection as in a mirror; then we shall see face to face. Now I know in part; then I shall know fully, even as I am fully known." In other words, one day we'll see how every piece of the puzzle fits together. But not while we're here on earth.

Finally, we need to hear and understand a valuable lesson that will shed light on the dark subject of death. The ultimate healing for a believer is death because it takes us into the presence of God. Remember, this life on earth is about loss. We lose our innocence, we lose our hearing, we lose our sight, and we lose our loved ones. The next life is about gain. The old things pass away, and all things are made new. It does not take the sting of death away, but it does give us hope. I know without hope, all is lost. With Christ, hope is enough.

Godspeed my friends.

Precious in the sight of the Lord is the death of his faithful servants.
                                    ~Psalm 116:15 NIV

START HERE...

Facing Life's Detours

Have you ever been late for an appointment or work and decided to take a shortcut through some backroads? Every time you've taken these streets, you've saved time. Except for this time. As you travel you see a sign which reads: "Detour straight ahead." Now you know there's no way to reach your final destination on time. How frustrating is that?

However, unexpected detours fill our life. You've finally saved enough money to take the vacation of a lifetime. However, the waterline in your house is busted. Detour straight ahead. You've looked forward to retirement all your life; now it's time to live a little bit. However, you find out your health is threatened by an unknown tumor. Detour straight ahead. Your child is about to graduate from high school, and you have all these plans for them to attend college. However, they break your heart by rebelling against those plans. Detour straight ahead. You and your spouse enjoy being with each other, and you are looking forward to growing old together. An unexpected call comes informing you of their death. Detour straight ahead. Your father or mother have always been your rock. Now they're having trouble remembering your name. Detour straight ahead. Life is full of unforeseen detours.

What do you do when, suddenly, your life experiences a detour? Well, it may sound simple, but you have to turn the navigation over to a higher power. God may not remove the detour, but He knows how to travel through it safely. Every time I have ventured from His pathway, He has safely brought me home. He will do the same for you. Of this I am sure. Safe travels.

Godspeed my friends.

> *Whether you turn to the right or to the left, your ears will hear a voice behind you, saying, "This is the way; walk in it."*
> ~Isaiah 30:21 NIV

START HERE...

Listen to the Warning

Over the last few days, the weathermen have warned us about the winter storm headed our way. This storm was supposed to bring freezing temperatures mixed with snow, sleet, and ice. Yesterday as our temperatures dropped to an "icy" fifty-five degrees, almost every school was already closed because of the potential for bad weather. (Long gone are the days that such decisions made the actual day that the storm hits. Dr. Marsh from the Cleveland School District would have waited until this morning after a drive through the city.) Nowadays the decision to cancel school is based upon the potential rather than actual. They err on the side of safety. I get it.

But there is another warning issued to all of us. It has not come from the National Weather Center, but rather from God. He has looked at the world which He created, and our wickedness has risen to His throne. The warning has come from His word, and that word is true. "If my people, who are called by name, will humble themselves and pray and seek my face and turn from their wicked ways, then I will hear from heaven, and I will forgive their sin and heal their land" (2 Chronicles 7:14 NIV). I wonder how many believers will heed this warning. The spiritual storm is upon us, and our only hope is in our God. But remember, it begins with his people being faithful.

Godspeed my friends.

> *Trust in the Lord with all your heart and lean not on your own understanding; in all your ways submit to him, and he will make your paths straight.*
>
> ~ Proverbs 3:5-6 NIV

START HERE...

No Hate Like Christian Hate

As we work our way toward Mother's Day, I want to share with you over the next few days lessons I learned from my mother. Mom would often say: "There's no hate quite like Christian hate!" As a pastor's wife, my mom saw firsthand the grumbling, fussing and fighting that often happened in church life. Where there are two Baptists, there will be four opinions. This was never clearer than was in the mid-seventies when my Dad led our church to an open-door policy. What this meant was, regardless of race, our church welcomed everyone. You might not think this was a big deal; well, it was a huge deal in the Mississippi Delta in the 1970s.

As a result of that decision, our church lost over a hundred members. Someone egged our house. They also destroyed our outside lamps. I remember sitting in my seventh-grade math class and having two former church members cast racial slurs in my direction. I recall going home and talking to my Mom about the situation. I can hear her now saying: "There's no hate quite like Christian hate."

I've been drawn back to that lesson over and over during my ministry. I've come to understand it more clearly as the years pass by. It's amazing to see how God's people treat those who have a different point of view than them. We're often quick to judge and slow to have compassion with those who are struggling in life. Remember the words of Billy Graham: "It's the Holy Spirit's job to convict, God's job to judge, and my job to love." Jesus reminds us that the world will know His disciples by how they love one another. Maybe the simple act of love is what's missing in so many lives and churches today. Lord knows we need His love now more than ever.

Godspeed my friends.

> *Above all, love each other deeply, because love covers over a multitude of sins.*
>
> ~1 Peter 4:8 NIV

START HERE...

Worry Changes Nothing

My mother was a chronic worrier. She worried about not having something about which to worry. One time I asked her: "When are you going to stop worrying about me?" Her reply was something I will never forget. She said: "The day I stop worrying about you is the day I draw my last breath." Most moms out there would echo her words when talking about their children. I've often wondered: "What are the mothers going to worry about when they get to Heaven?" There's a difference in unnecessary worry and loving concern about your children. We need to have a healthy balance.

Worry is interest on a note before it comes due. Unnecessary worry will rob you of the joy of this day. There is a simple formula that I've used over the years. It has become so common that often some of my church members throw it up in my face and remind me of that same philosophy. "If you can change it, then change it. If you can't change it, then don't worry about it." Many of us would do well to follow this simple reminder in life.

Worry is counterproductive. You can't add one minute to your life by worrying. Just the opposite takes place. We take time off of our life by worrying. It's also a form of atheism. When we worry about life, we demonstrate that we do not truly believe the promises of God. Don't let the worries of life rob you of the joy God wants you to experience this day; for to miss the joy is to miss everything.

Godspeed my friends.

> *But seek first his kingdom and his righteousness, and all these things will be given to you as well. Therefore do not worry about tomorrow, for tomorrow will worry about itself. Each day has enough trouble of its own.*
> ~Matthew 6:33-34 NIV

START HERE...

Do Not Miss the Blessings

Yesterday morning I selected my coffee pod and placed it in the Keurig machine like I've done hundreds of times before, and walked away. As I looked back at the coffee maker, I noticed something was missing. I had forgotten to place my coffee mug under the stream of freshly brewed java. In a mad hurry, I frantically searched for a mug. When I finally had the mug in place, and the coffee was completely brewed, only about a fourth of the cup was full. The rest had drained in the chamber below. (By the way, the collection area is larger than it used to be. In my old one coffee would have run over on to the counters. How do I know that? A friend told me.) What a waste of a perfectly good cup of coffee.

Likewise, every day God is pouring out his blessings, and the problem for many of us is, our mugs are not in place. We've become too distracted by the worries and cares of the world, and we miss the blessings of a loving Heavenly Father. I believe, without a shadow of a doubt, that one day I'll stand before God and he will say: "Why didn't you let me bless you more?" Then I fear He will walk me into a room filled with unclaimed blessings on my life. How does this happen in life? Pretty simple; we take our eyes off of that which should be central, and we miss the blessings.

How about you today? Is your mug in place to receive the flow of God's blessings on your life? God loves you and wants to pour out His blessings upon you today. However, you must be in a position to receive them.

Godspeed my friends.

> *For I know the plans I have for you," declares the Lord, "plans to prosper you and not to harm you, plans to give you hope and a future.*
>
> ~Jeremiah 29:11 NIV

START HERE...

When Life Piles On

There are times, for all of us, when life seems to pile upon us. No matter what we do, we can't seem to catch a break. When things start heading south, it's hard to turn it around. It's like a snowball going downhill; it just keeps getting bigger and bigger. The reality is, no one is immune from this problem.

Life piles up on us financially. Most of us know what it's like to have more month than money. Everything hits at once. April is certainly a pile-on month for me. For me, my annual taxes and my estimated quarterly taxes are both due on the same day. But for others out there, your home air conditioning and car tires both need to be replaced at the same time. That's not even mentioning the bill that is due to the orthodontist; and by the way, you need to pay for your season football tickets. It's enough to put anyone in the tank.

Life piles on us physically. If you live long enough, you'll find that your body starts breaking down. Just with regular visits to the doctor, optometrist, and dentist, it's hard to keep up. You are not even taking into account your sleep study, orthopedic visit, and dermatologist appointment. You know you're getting old when your social calendar revolves around your doctor's appointments.

Life piles up on us spiritually as well. We seem to get hit from every direction. We try to do the right thing, but instead of getting easier, life gets harder. We have a prodigal child, a death in the family, or a broken relationship. We feel cold and alone, and we cry out to God: "Where are you? If you're not going to work with me, then don't work against me!"

When life piles on, stop for a moment and breathe. Remember the promise of your God: "I will never leave or forsake you." You'll find when life piles on, there's a protective layer between you and life. That, my friends, is the presence of God. He is with you, even in the piles of life.

Godspeed my friends.

The Lord himself goes before you and will be with you; he will never leave you nor forsake you. Do not be afraid; do not be discouraged.

~Deuteronomy 31:8 NIV

START HERE...

The Time to Prepare is Now

Several months ago, the doctor scheduled Doug for fairly serious surgery. He was so convinced that he wouldn't live through the procedure that he made a point to visit with every significant person in his life before his surgery. His visits eventually led him to my office. We talked and prayed together. Not only did he make it through that surgery, but he also made it through a second procedure. But he didn't want to leave any stone uncovered. You see, he was a farmer by trade, and he knew the importance of hard work and preparation. I told him after his second surgery: "You fooled us all and survived to live another day." But he didn't take the chance of not doing what he needed to do.

Yesterday morning while driving his tractor down Highway 82, Doug was hit from behind by a truck and was killed. After surviving two surgeries in the last six months, he died unexpectedly and tragically. But he also died prepared. You see, he had said what he needed to say. He had done what he needed to do. The farmer who had given up his vocation and passion, died doing what he loved to do. It was an unexplainable accident, plain and simple. But if anyone was ready, it was Doug. There are no more fields to be turned. There are no more crops to be planted. Just a crown of righteousness to be received.

You never know about tomorrow. If I were you, I'd live like I was dying and do what I needed to do. Doug sure did.

Godspeed my friends.

> *Get ready; be prepared, you and all the hordes gathered about you, and take command of them.*
>
> ~Ezekiel 38:7 NIV

START HERE...

God is Present Even in the Silence

A couple of weeks ago, I was in my front yard picking up trash. For some reason, my yard serves as a giant garbage can for all those who pass by my house. As I made my way across the slope on my lawn, I noticed something unusual. There were deer tracks in a muddy section of my yard. One night a huge deer walked from the other side of the road straight through my yard and right beside my house. In the six plus years that we've lived here, I've never once seen a deer on my property. However, the tracks prove that indeed they have not only been here, but they've been close.

In a similar sense, throughout my life, there have been moments when I've questioned the presence of God. I've wondered where He has been in the midst of my pain, grief, suffering, and aloneness. For all of us, there are moments in our spiritual journey when we ask God: "Are you with me and do you even care about me?" When one is struggling in the darkness, it's hard not to feel isolated and abandoned. Some of the greatest saints who ever walked the face of the earth have felt the same way. Those heroes include Elijah, Jeremiah, Job, and even John the Baptist.

However, when we stop for a moment and look back, we see His footprints all over our lives and circumstances. Even when we didn't see Him or feel Him, He was there. The tracks of His footprints prove that over and over. He never promised us a life free from heartache and pain, but He has promised us that nothing will separate us from His love and presence. Look back. You will see that His tracks made all the difference.

Godspeed my friends.

You will seek me and find me when you seek me with all your heart.

~Jeremiah 29:13 NIV

START HERE...

Who is the GOAT?

Have you ever heard the term GOAT? I have to be honest; several years ago I had to google the meaning of this capitalized word. I was familiar with the word "scapegoat," and given a chance, I could make you a list of folks who acted like an "old goat." But, how others were using GOAT was new to me. The term GOAT is an acronym for "The Greatest of All Time." For the most part, it is an expression used in sports. It denotes the greatest player to play a certain sport. For instance, many think Michael Jordan and Tom Brady are the GOATs of their specific disciplines. The problem with making such a claim is, it's always subjective. Everyone has their own opinion.

But on the other hand, when you talk about the greatest person who ever lived, there is no debate. It is quite simple. The answer is overwhelmingly obvious. It is Jesus Christ. From his birth to his death, he demonstrated the qualities of greatness. But what made him so unique is that the greatness he demonstrated was not for his glory, but rather for the glory of the Father. In other words, it was a life that reflected the love, grace, and mercy of a loving God.

The good news for us is when we accept His free gift of salvation, we share in His greatness. What Jesus did, what He said, how He lived and why He died, was for you and me. Furthermore, He calls us to live a life of greatness through service and faith. Remember, God judges greatness much differently than the world. We can't share in His suffering, but we can share in His victory. The Greatest of All Time calls us to join Him on a journey and life of greatness. Don't you think it is time you joined Him and lived up to His standards? He is waiting.

Godspeed my friends.

The Word became flesh and made his dwelling among us. We have seen his glory, the glory of the one and only Son, who came from the Father, full of grace and truth.
~John 1:14 NIV

START HERE...

Is God Pleased with Our Effort?

I saw a press conference yesterday from a college basketball coach following his team's twenty-point win against their arch rival on the road. His team is currently undefeated and ranked second in the nation, but to hear him talk, you'd think they hadn't won a game. He said: "If we think we're going to win a conference championship, we're kidding ourselves. We're not tough enough mentally. We have to get some things settled among ourselves if we're going to be successful." You see, the great ones are never satisfied with just winning, it's about getting better every day. Talent will only take you so far.

I wonder what kind of press conference God would hold to discuss our performances? It might sound something like this: "I know our kids are showing up for worship and Bible study. They are even making an effort to give financially to the Kingdom. But I'm worried about their hearts. They have too many distractions in their daily lives. They are neglecting the things that matter. Their prayer life and personal Bible study are lacking. I can't remember the last time they shared their faith with anyone. Even when they're at church, their minds are somewhere else. They worry about the trivial things in life and fail to realize how blessed they are. I wish they would give a better effort each day. If they think the world is going to get better without their help, they are kidding themselves. If only they would humble themselves, pray, and seek me. Then I would hear their prayers and heal their land."

Maybe we need to look at our own lives and how well we're measuring up. I cannot believe that God is very pleased with what He is seeing. The Great One never is.

Godspeed my friends.

For this reason, since the day we heard about you, we have not stopped praying for you. We continually ask God to fill you with the knowledge of his will through all the wisdom and understanding that the Spirit gives.

~Colossians 1:9 NIV

START HERE...

Putting the Pieces Back Together

They say that time heals a broken heart. However, there are some hurts, pains, and brokenness that even time cannot heal. On the other hand, time does allow us the opportunity to adjust to the pain. Time gives us the chance to move on and not dwell on the pain. Time gives us a chance to pick up the pieces of our lives and make something of them. There are times in those dark moments when we learn more about ourselves and our Creator. One valuable lesson we need to remember is: "Even though it may seem like it, we're never alone."

Is your life shattered into pieces? If so, where do you turn? Well, if your house was ripped apart due to a storm, I'm sure you'd call a carpenter. Well, if you'll remember, Jesus, by trade, was a carpenter. He knew how to fix a chair long before he became a traveling preacher. Throughout his ministry, we noticed how he was an expert in putting lives back together; broken lives, that is. If you are experiencing brokenness, you might want to consider talking to him. He can heal the broken heart. He alone can make all the difference in your life. What do you have to lose?

Godspeed my friends.

He heals the brokenhearted and binds up their wounds.
                                                            ~Psalm 147:3 NIV

START HERE...

Face Forward, Please

It's a big day in a toddler's life when his car seat is turned to face forward. For over a year, that child has only seen where he has been rather than where he is going. For the first time, he can see Mom and Dad and not just hear their voices. It is hard for us to imagine the excitement in his life when his entire perspective changes with just a simple adjustment to his car seat. Now all things are new every time he takes a ride. I would think this thought has to run through his mind: "So this is what I've been missing!"

The same is true with our own lives. Far too many of us are living in the past. We are concentrating on where we've been, what we've done, and who we were. We continue to hold on to the victories, the defeats, the pain, and the misery of the past. The problem with this philosophy is it robs you of the joy of today. Listen closely. You are not what you used to be. Thank God, you are not what you are going to be.

Don't you think it's time you made a simple adjustment in your vantage point on life? It's time to stop harboring feelings of resentment, regret, shame, and guilt. God desires to make all things new in your life. The old can pass away, and the new has infinite possibilities for an abundant life. The only thing holding you back is your pride and resentment. The choice is yours. Stop looking back at where you've been and start looking forward to where God is leading you. Imagine the excitement that awaits you today and every day. Turn the seat around.

Godspeed my friends.

> Jesus replied, "No one who puts a hand to the plow and looks back is fit for service in the kingdom of God."
> ~Luke 9:62 NIV

START HERE...

Are You Reflecting the Love of Christ?

The other night, while we were eating in a local restaurant, a lady came up to our table and asked me: "Are you the guy I see running each morning around the Pleasant Hill area?" I replied: "Yes, I am." She went on to say: "I'm the bus driver that passes you each morning." A little later, I went up to her table and asked her: "Do you have any trouble seeing me in the mornings?" I'm always concerned about my safety with oncoming traffic. I wear a reflective vest and a flashlight on my cap. She smiled and said: "I can see your reflection from that vest for miles."

I thought about what she said for a couple of days: "I can see your reflection from that vest for miles." In a real sense, shouldn't the world see the reflection of Christ in our lives each day? In our workplace, shouldn't others see Jesus in our actions? At school, our friends and teachers should see the radiant reflection of the Father in our lives. Every day we are a witness or a reflection of something or someone. Your actions and words will always betray you or give credence to your faith. Be careful and concerned about what reflection your life is sending to others.

What are you reflecting today in your life? I'd never noticed the driver of that school bus, but she noticed and saw me. You better believe the world is noticing you. Reflect Christ and all He stands for each day.

Godspeed my friends.

And we all, who with unveiled faces contemplate the Lord's glory, are being transformed into his image with ever-increasing glory, which comes from the Lord, who is the Spirit.
~2 Corinthians 3:18 NIV

START HERE...

Expect the Unexpected

Have you ever considered how quickly your life can change? In just a matter of minutes or hours, you can go from the highest of the highs to the lowest of the lows. It happened to me in August 2007. On Sunday night we celebrated an installation service at our new place of ministry only to learn twelve hours later that my mother had passed away. You talk about emotional extremes – I am not sure I have ever gone from one hundred miles per hour to zero so fast. Everything changed, and not for the good.

Similarly, the same thing happened in the life of our Lord and Savior over two thousand years ago. On Palm Sunday He entered the Holy City of Jerusalem to the shouts of the people: "Hosanna! Blessed is He who comes in the name of the Lord!" It was a cry of "Save us now!" A few days later Jesus was betrayed by a friend, denied by one of His closest companions, accused of a crime He never committed and abandoned by His followers. Ultimately, as if He were a common criminal, Jesus was executed. He was hailed one minute and nailed the next. However, Jesus had prepared for the journey.

When life stops on a dime and does a complete 180, will you be prepared? I can tell you this, the events of life will either draw you closer to God or move you farther away from His felt presence. This week is Holy Week. It is time to prepare yourself for whatever life deals you. Ready or not, it is going to happen. So you need to begin by walking hand in hand with the Savior.

Godspeed my friends.

> *Now listen, you who say, "Today or tomorrow we will go to this or that city, spend a year there, carry on business and make money." Why, you do not even know what will happen tomorrow. What is your life? You are a mist that appears for a little while and then vanishes.*
>
> *~James 4:13-14 NIV*

START HERE...

You Think You Have It Bad

I had a former church member who would often say: "If we all got into a room, and everyone threw their troubles out on the table, and you saw what other people were going through, you would quickly pick up your own." All of us are dealing with something in our lives, and no one is exempt. In the book of Job, we are reminded: "Yet man is born to trouble as surely as sparks fly upward" (Job 5:7 NIV). However, the evil one will whisper in your ear that you are alone, and everyone else has their lives altogether. Don't believe the lie.

Every Sunday I have the unique opportunity to preach the word of God to a group of people I love. As I gaze out at the congregation, I'm aware of some of the hurts and pains they are dealing with daily. Some are suffering physically, while others are dealing with emotional problems. Some are dealing with family issues, while others are struggling to make it financially. The feelings of inadequacy and aloneness often compound the struggles. They want relief, but for some reason, it is slow to arrive. It's hard to hear another person say: "Hang in there. Things will get better." Too often we're not sure how better looks.

I heard an old preacher say his favorite verse in the Bible was: "It came to pass." He went on to say: "Notice, it doesn't say it came to stay." Remember, the sun still shines somewhere, even when it's raining. Learn that while you're in the storm of life, you are not alone. Sometimes that can be the real difference maker. I know it is in my life.

Godspeed my friends.

> *I have told you these things, so that in me you may have peace. In this world you will have trouble. But take heart! I have overcome the world.*
>
> ~John 16:33 NIV

START HERE...

The Church Still Matters

Last night I was preaching on the story of Ruth out of the Old Testament. It's a beautiful story of love, devotion, and loyalty. There are moments in my own life when I read the words Ruth spoke to her mother-in-law, Naomi, and my emotions get the best of me. "Where you go, I will go, and where you stay, I will stay. Your people will be my people and your God my God. Where you die, I will die, and there I will be buried" (Ruth 1:16b-17a NIV). Can you imagine the love, commitment, and loyalty Ruth demonstrated to one who was not even part of her immediate family? It reminds us all that we do not have to be blood kin to be family.

In my life, I've had the honor of establishing friendships with individuals who have become more than friends. They have become family. They have become fathers, mothers, sisters, brothers, sons, and daughters to me. Along the way, some have even become like grandchildren in my eyes. The family of God is like that. It brings certain people into our lives at the right time, and they change the course of our lives. They have helped me in my darkest hours, and they have rejoiced with me in my highest moments. No one has been more blessed than me through these relationships.

When individuals tell me that the church is no longer relevant and is out of date, I remind them of the blessings we all receive when we invest in one another's lives. There is no telling where I would be today without the love and acceptance I've known over the years at a place called "church." There are no people like God's people.

Godspeed my friends.

> *Every day they continued to meet together in the temple courts. They broke bread in their homes and ate together with glad and sincere hearts, praising God and enjoying the favor of all the people. And the Lord added to their number daily those who were being saved.*
>
> ~Acts 2:46-47 NIV

START HERE...

You Are Not That Bad

Today as the family and friends of Billy Graham gather to pay their last respects to him, I can't help but think about the message of hope and love he preached regularly. I can hear him now: "I don't care what you've done or where you've been; I only know that God loves you and wants to save you by faith." That's a message many of us preachers need to remember and proclaim to our congregations.

There are times when people do not need to be reminded how bad they are; most already know. They need to hear how loving and accepting God is to all people. I may be talking to some of you today. Somehow, some way, you have become convinced that you have walked beyond the grace and forgiveness of God. I'm here to tell you that there's no place that far. All you need to do is ask God for forgiveness and accept his free gift of love and salvation. Scripture tells us: "If we confess our sins, he is faithful and just and will forgive us our sins and purify us from all unrighteousness" (1 John 1:9 NIV). The choice is yours to make.

Now understand this: the evil one will do all he can to convince you this is impossible because of the things you've done in the past. Remember, he is a liar, and his sole purpose is to steal, kill, and destroy. God's plan for your life is to bless it as you submit your life to Him. Today, if you hear his voice, harden not your heart. Just read John 3:16. The world includes you and me. Hallelujah, what a Savior!

Godspeed my friends.

> *For God so loved the world that he gave his one and only Son, that whoever believes in him shall not perish but have eternal life.*
>
> ~John 3:16 NIV

START HERE...

Marriage is More Important Than the Wedding

The other night while I was attending a Mississippi State basketball game, a beautiful young mother of two, who had been one of our youth members at a church I previously served, came and sat behind me. Years ago, it had been my honor to perform her wedding. As her husband made his way to his seat and got situated, I asked them: "Is that knot I tied still tight?" With a godly smile on her face, she responded: "Tighter than ever. By the way, how many weddings have you done over the years?" I told her I had no clue because it never dawned on me to keep such a record. It blessed my heart to see how this couple has grown in their love for each other as they continue to establish Christ as the head of their house.

We're about to head into the spring and summer months of the year, and a lot of couples will celebrate their wedding day. Over the years, weddings have changed quite a bit. I can't remember the last time I attended a wedding reception where there was a cake, a bowl full of mixed nuts, and a tray of pastel mints to go along with some green punch. The average cost of a wedding these days is $27,000. Let that sink in for a moment. The problem many couples have is they spend so much time planning for their wedding, that they forget to prepare for the marriage. The wedding and reception last just a few hours. After throwing the rice, the honeymoon begins. But, even that comes to an end. At some point, you have to come home to begin living life together.

The best advice I could give to a young couple is to prepare more for the marriage than the wedding. This preparation should always include premarital counseling with a pastor or a Christian counselor. No matter the cost, or the time, this is a must. Also, couples need to set as a priority a religious ritual in their home. In other words, find a church home and grow in your faith together. Remember: "Unless the Lord builds a house, the builders labor in vain" (Psalm 127:1a NIV). I wonder how many of the marriages I've performed are still growing strong? Of the ones that are, I can assure you, Christ is involved in that relationship. If not, it's still not too late.

Godspeed my friends.

> *Love is patient, love is kind. It does not envy, it does not boast, it is not proud. It does not dishonor others, it is not self-seeking, it is not easily angered, it keeps no record of wrongs. Love does not delight in evil but rejoices with the truth. It always protects, always trusts, always hopes, always perseveres.*
>
> ~1 Corinthians 13:4-7 NIV

START HERE...

Forgiveness is a Slippery Slope

Every now and then I get an inbox on messenger from one of my friends on Facebook. In these messages, some people are asking for prayer about certain situations they're going through, while others are seeking advice about problems they are facing in life. I am probably the least qualified to deal with certain things, but, hopefully, God uses something I say or write to help these individuals. One question someone recently asked me was: "How do you get over hurtful things done by family members even when they refuse to apologize? And furthermore, they keep doing the same thing over and over."

Forgiveness is a slippery slope in the Christian life. Our forgiveness from God is tied directly to our willingness to forgive others. The reality of the situation is, those who hurt us, rarely come and apologize for their actions. Sadder still, this often happens in the church. Some of the most devastating things which have taken place in my life and the life of my family have come through the actions and words of church folks. When this happens, I have two choices. First, I can become angry and allow an unforgiving spirit to fester in my heart. When I do this, it cuts me off from the presence of God. It will also affect other relationships as well.

Second, I can forgive that person and move on with my life. You've heard the expression: "Forgive and forget." That's humanly impossible. But you can forgive and get on with your life. Don't expect ungodly people to act godly. Even in family situations, you can love them, but not allow them to continue to hurt you. Sometimes limited exposure is best. Give it time. Maybe, just maybe, their hearts will change. Pray for God to work in their hearts. But hear this: "Life is too short for unhealthy relationships." You decide how much time to invest. I'm not Dr. Phil, but I want to surround myself with people who elevate me spiritually, mentally, emotionally, and socially. I do not need to be around those who continually tear me down. Hopefully, this is of some help to you today.

Godspeed my friends.

> *Be kind and compassionate to one another, forgiving each other, just as in Christ God forgave you.*
> ~Ephesians 4:32 NIV

START HERE...

Yes, I Talk to Jesus Regularly

I don't know if you've noticed, but the individuals who scream at the top of their lungs about tolerance and acceptance are the most intolerant people around. Furthermore, they feel they can say anything they want about another person because it's their right and privilege. Heaven help those who profess Jesus Christ as their Lord and Savior because our culture will be mock and ridicule them publicly and regularly.

This past week on the television show "The View," Joy Behar, one of the hosts, suggested that Vice President Mike Pence has to be "mentally ill" because he not only talks to Jesus, but he listens to Him as well. I can tell you without reservation, that if any celebrity criticized or mocked an individual of the Islamic, the LBGTQ community, or any other group, disciplinary action would have been swift and severe. But why are we surprised by such events? These things have happened because Christian people have become lackadaisical about their walk with God. Maybe we haven't been listening to Him enough.

Ms. Behar does not understand Christianity. Our faith in Christ Jesus gives us direct access to the Father. When we pray, we go directly into the presence of our Creator. And prayer my friends, is a dialogue, not a monologue, with God. We speak to Him, and He speaks to us. It's called living by the Spirit. But don't expect the world to understand it. Remember, Jesus said that the world would mock and ridicule us for our beliefs.

Another aspect of our faith is forgiveness. We not only have to love one another, but we are commanded to forgive and pray for those who persecute us. So today, I forgive Ms. Behar for her hurtful and misinformed words. I hope she learned a lesson about tolerance.

I can't help but be reminded of this chorus:

And He walks with me
And He talks with me
And He tells me I am his own
And the joy we share as we tarry there
None other has ever known

Count me among the mentally ill, for His voice I often hear. Godspeed my friends.

Rejoice always, pray continually, give thanks in all circumstances; for this is God's will for you in Christ Jesus.
~1 Thessalonians 5:16-18 NIV

START HERE...

Don't Expect the World to Act Godly

In light of the most recent mass school shooting that left seventeen high school students dead, many of us are left wondering how this has now become commonplace in our country. Over the past few days, so many of us have offered solutions to a problem which is now at epidemic proportions. What drove Nikolas Cruz to take an AR-15 assault rifle, walk down a hallway, and end the lives of these innocent, precious young people? Upon his arrest, the FBI agents and police officers said he had a cold and strange look on his face. One would have to expect he was driven by evil forces to do such a thing. The reality of the world in which we live is, there are still a lot of individuals out there like Cruz who are waiting for their chance to inflict needless pain on others. How have we arrived at such a place in our society?

This past month a group of men from our church security team attended a seminar on church safety. The speaker told the attendees that on average there are four acts of violence each month in churches around our nation. Think about that for a moment. Two places where we've always assumed we'd be safe, our schools and our churches, have become places of uncertainty and violence. At our church, we take extra precautions every time we have a service because that's the world in which we now live.

Now I'm not for a moment going to suggest that I have an answer to this horrific situation. But I am going to say that God's people have to step up and get serious about our responsibilities. How can we expect the world to act godly when the church, the bride of Christ, is not? Somehow, we have taken our eyes off of the main thing and have gotten sidetracked from our mission. We have been called to be the light of the world by our love for one another. Now if we can't get that right, how are we going to change the world? Christians have a hard time loving those with whom we disagree. The solution for a troubled world is changed hearts among

God's people. We better start remembering what is important. Do you know what it is?

"Jesus replied, 'Love the Lord your God with all your heart and with all your soul and with all your mind. This is the first and greatest commandment. And the second is like it: Love your neighbor as yourself'" (Matthew 22:37-39 NIV). Everything hinges on that: loving God and loving others. It's time to set pettiness aside and get serious about serving God. You say that's a dream and an unreal proposition to a complex situation. I say it's a mandate given to us by Jesus Himself. But then again, I am a simple guy, but I serve a mighty God. He must become the focal point of everything a believer does.

Godspeed my friends.

> *I have told you these things, so that in me you may have peace. In this world you will have trouble. But take heart! I have overcome the world.*
>
> ~John 16:33 NIV

START HERE...

Get Up and Press On

This morning I got up a bit earlier to head out on a long run. About a half mile into my journey I felt a sharp pain in the back of my leg. It was as if someone had shot me. The pain was so great that it took me to the ground. Immediately, there was no doubt in my mind what had taken place; I had pulled my hamstring. While I was lying on the ground, to make matters worse, it started raining. Okay, what do you do? You do the best that you can. You get up and try to get home. A million things rush through your mind, and, of course, there's a life lesson here for us all.

There are times in life when you are rocking along pretty good, and suddenly, out of nowhere, something or someone knocks you to the ground. The pain in your heart is excruciating. You are broken, battered, and hurting. What do you do? Some choose to stay down and wallow in self-pity. But you have to get up and keep on keeping on in life. You can't let the fall define your life. The good news is, you get to choose.

Second, when the pain is at its greatest, and you don't think it can get worse, don't be surprised by the rain and the storms which follow. The external noise around you will make the journey harder than you imagined. But remember, the trip home takes place one step at a time. This morning, to be honest, I wasn't sure if I'd make it back to the house, but I did, one step at a time.

Now there's a choice in my life. My leg is killing me now. What am I going to do about it? The answer is simple: I will rehab my leg and get healthy. I assure you that I will run again very soon. There is not another option. The same is true in life. You have to get up, get healthy, and live again. If it were easy, everyone would do it. You must decide to press on. Will there be additional pain? You bet. But in the end, it will be worth it. It will be for you as well. The rehab starts today for me. When does it start for you?

Godspeed my friends.

To this you were called, because Christ suffered for you, leaving you an example, that you should follow in his steps.
~1 Peter 2:21 NIV

START HERE...

The Disease That No One is Addressing

I cannot remember a flu season like we have experienced this year. According to health experts, this is the worst outbreak of influenza in the thirteen years they have been tracking it. Over twelve thousand individuals have been hospitalized, and tragically, it has claimed the lives of over thirty children. Because it's so widespread, all you have to do is to come in contact with one who is infected, and there's a good chance you'll end up sick. Please, by all means, do your best to take the necessary precautions to stay healthy.

However, there's another disease out there today that's just as widespread and just as dangerous. It may not claim your life, but it can change your disposition and color your soul black. It's the disease of negativity, and it's widespread in our schools, homes, and churches. All you have to do is come in contact with one who is infected and, before you know it, it is changing you. Our society is full of individuals who can tell you everything that's wrong with our world, nation, city, and even our churches. They are the experts in fault finding and judgment. As you associate with them, they start infecting you. They gripe a lot, but rarely offer any solutions to our problems.

Be careful of the company you keep because your actions will soon mirror the people around you. I can stand to be around a negative person for about thirty seconds. Any longer and there must be an escape plan. Do not fall victim to this disease. With the proper treatment and correct time of rest, you can conquer the flu. Negativity can last years and rob a person of his joy in life. There is no vaccine for this disease. I've known folks who could stand a double dose. Today, I choose joy and happiness. Hopefully, you will too. Don't let the Scrooges of life infect your heart. Life is too short to be miserable every day.

Godspeed my friends.

Finally, brothers and sisters, whatever is true, whatever is noble, whatever is right, whatever is pure, whatever is lovely, whatever is admirable—if anything is excellent or praiseworthy—think about such things.

~Philippians 4:8 NIV

START HERE...

Important Life Lessons

In my fifty-eight plus years on this earth, I have learned some valuable lessons. It is impossible to give a comprehensive list; but, allow me to share with you three things that can help you live productively as a child of God.

The first lesson I learned at an early age, and it is still true today, is that LIFE IS NOT FAIR. If you are looking for "fair," you might want to check out a place with a merry-go-round or Ferris wheel. The sooner you learn this lesson, the quicker you can move on in life.

Second, LIFE IS UNPREDICTABLE. The moment you think you have everything figured out, things change. Never say: "Nothing surprises me," because, I can assure you, something will. Your life can change for the better or worse in a matter minutes. Always expect the unexpected.

Finally, LIFE IS BRIEF. Isn't it amazing how fast the days go by the older that we get? James compared our life to a vapor that is here one minute and gone the next. So, with that in mind, you better make your life count. Give it to something that will outlast you.

Godspeed my friends.

> *For whoever wants to save their life will lose it, but whoever loses their life for me will find it.*
>
> ~Matthew 16:25 NIV

START HERE...

Everybody Has a Plan

Former heavyweight boxing champion Mike Tyson once said: "Everyone has a plan until they get punched in the mouth." At the time, he didn't know how true that statement would be in life as well. Everyone knows how they'd handle a particular situation until that situation comes into their life. We tend to set ourselves up for a fall when we say: "Well I can tell you how I'd handle that problem." Then suddenly we get punched in the mouth by life, and things don't look the same. Why is that?

We need to realize that we don't have all the facts about another person's life and struggles. We might think we know, but we don't. Every life and problem is different and carries with it different circumstances. For instance, a young girl finds herself pregnant in the middle of her high school years. Her parents handle the situation as best as they can. It's easy to sit on the sidelines and say: "Well, I can tell you how I'd have dealt with it!" Really? How do you know until you've faced the same thing?

We see someone struggling following the death of a loved one, and we think: "What's their problem? Why can't they snap out of it? If that were me, I'd be over it by now." Really? Be careful what you say, for you might soon find yourself facing the same grief.

Every life is different, and how we handle certain problems are as unique as our personalities. Instead of sitting in judgment of another person's response to a calamity in life, why don't you sit with them? Sometimes a hurting soul doesn't want advice; they want a shoulder to lean on in troubled times. Your plan may work better, but that's not the point. Are you willing to lighten the burden another is bearing? When we do, we become the hands and feet of Christ. That is more important than your plan.

Godspeed my friends.

For by the grace given me I say to every one of you: Do not think of yourself more highly than you ought, but rather think of yourself with sober judgment, in accordance with the faith God has distributed to each of you.

~Romans 12:3 NIV

START HERE...

Sympathy or Empathy ... There is a Big Difference

How many times have you been with a friend, neighbor, coworker, or fellow church member who has recently gone through a crisis in their life? Maybe they've lost a loved one; a spouse, a parent, or Heaven forbid, a child. It could be that this individual has been diagnosed with cancer or some other life-threatening disease. As you leave their presence you utter these words: "If we can do anything for you, let us know." We have all repeated that sentence at one time or another. But here's the reality. 99.9 percent of the hurting people are not going to call you. You know it, and for the most part, they know it, as well.

Several years ago, following a catastrophic event in a church member's life, I had an interesting conversation with them. They were struggling physically, emotionally, and financially. They had plenty of money, but they were overwhelmed at the decisions they had to make. I asked them if they had asked anyone to help them, and I was shocked into reality with their response. "People say nice things when the crisis occurs, and then they disappear." There's a lot of truth in that thought process.

There is a difference between sympathy and empathy. Empathy is sympathy with shoes. Empathy does not wait to be asked to help; it just helps. Today, don't forget about the hurting and the grieving. Most people will not ask for assistance. So instead of asking what you can do for someone, look around and find something that needs doing. Does their yard need to be mowed? Then mow it. Lighten their load. They will be grateful, and you will be blessed.

Godspeed my friends.

> *If anyone has material possessions and sees a brother or sister in need but has no pity on them, how can the love of God be in that person?*
>
> ~1 John 3:17 NIV

START HERE...

All Things Work Together

One of my favorite verses in the Bible is Romans 8:28: "And we know that in all things God works for the good of those who love him, who have been called according to his purpose" (NIV). That passage of scripture has seen me through some of the most difficult days in my life. However, there are a couple of things we need to know about this verse for us to fully understand it and allow it to speak to us when we are hurting.

First, this scripture doesn't say that everything which happens to us is good. What is good about the death of a loved one? What is good about a rebellious child? What is good about the loss of a job? What is good about the dark night of the soul when you question everything about religion and God himself? The answer is quite simple: not a single thing. The reality of life is that bad things happen which have absolutely nothing to do with the will of God. They come as a result of our free will to make decisions on our own. However, God takes the blame for a lot of things for which He is innocent.

Second, and most important, understand the true meaning of this verse. How I interpret the verse helps me understand a lot about the love of God. Somehow, some way behind the curtains of life, God is working in every situation to bring about something good. Furthermore, understand this: you may not even see the good this side of Heaven. Why is that? Because in this life, we only see in part. But one day, we will see everything and how each piece of the puzzle fits together. I know it doesn't make the pain go away or ease the current burden, but it does give me hope.

When times are hard, and the nights are long, cling to that which you know and to the One you know. You don't have to have all the answers; hold fast to the One who does. It will make a difference. How do I know this? It has been proven over and over in my life. And if you look back, it will be true in your life, as well.

Godspeed my friends.

And we know that in all things God works for the good of those who love him, who have been called according to his purpose.
~Romans 8:28 NIV

START HERE...

The Blessings of a Parent

There is one thing every child wants from his parents. It seems as though it would easily be bestowed upon him at his birth, but so often a child will search near and far but never receive it. More than anything else, a child wants the blessings of his parents. He wants to know that he is loved and accepted just as he is. The sad reality is even adult children long to know they are "alright" in the eyes of their mother and father.

I can't tell you how many young men or young ladies have sat in my office during a premarital session and suddenly broken down at the realization that their parents have never said to them: "I love you." The emotional scars from the past are often still raw and painful in the present.

Before my parents' marriage, to the best of my understanding, my dad was not an affectionate individual. All that changed when he married my mom, whose father was a full-blooded Frenchman. My mother turned him into an affectionate individual. There was never a time that I talked to him on the phone that he didn't end the conversation by telling me he loved me. Whenever I would see him, you could rest assured that he'd hug or even kiss me. As a fifteen-year-old it was embarrassing, but as I grew older, it was something I longed for in my life.

Don't assume your children know how you feel about them merely based on what you provide for them. Your actions, good or bad, will speak volumes about your love and acceptance of your children. So, what are you waiting for my friend? Tell your children that you love them as they are. You might not think it's important, but I can assure you, they are longing for that affirmation.

Godspeed my friends.

> *As a father has compassion on his children, so the Lord has compassion on those who fear him.*
> ~Psalm 103:13 NIV

START HERE...

The Storms Are Sure to Come

Are you ready for the storm? I'm not talking about the forecast for the next few days, but rather the storm that may hit your life this year. You've heard it over and over again. There are three types of people: those in the midst of a storm, those coming out of a storm, and those about to go through a storm. In a message I shared with our people Sunday night, I said: "The very thing you prize the most in life can be taken from you at any given moment." So again, the question is asked: "Are you ready for the storm?"

You don't wait until you're in the air to learn to fly the plane. You don't wait until you're in the middle of the ocean before you learn to swim. You don't wait until the test is handed out to start studying for the quiz. And you don't wait until disaster hits to prepare yourself spiritually for the recovery. How you and I handle the catastrophes of life says more about our faith than anything.

Sunday morning, I walked into our senior adult men's Bible study group. As I opened the door, all of their heads were bowed in a moment of prayer. The one voicing the prayer was the man who had just buried his wife the day before after seventy years of marriage. You don't think that spoke volumes about his life and his faith. He was prepared for the storm.

In order to prepare yourself, you must be prayed up. A regular time of prayer and communion with God gives us a sense of peace, knowing we're not alone. Too often we limit our prayer life to asking God for certain things. Start each day with a time of prayer.

Second, spend time in God's word. Many of us are willing to defend or debate the Word of God, but yet we do not read His Word regularly. When we spend time in the Bible, we see that our spiritual heroes were as dysfunctional as us. We also learn more about the promises and love of God. I can't tell you how many times a passage of scripture has spoken to me at the time I needed it the most.

Finally, find a support group at a local church. A community of faith can encourage you. Other believers can help bear the burdens of life. Trust me, the coal that burns in isolation will soon turn cold. We need each other because this world is tough and unpredictable.

So, I'll ask you again. Are you ready? Don't wait until the storm hits to begin the preparation. By then, it will be too late.

Godspeed my friends.

> *So do not fear, for I am with you; do not be dismayed, for I am your God. I will strengthen you and help you; I will uphold you with my righteous right hand.*
>
> ~Isaiah 41:10 NIV

START HERE...

The Greatest of These Is Love

Every now and then, in my profession, I get to witness love in its purest form. You see the love between two people as God intended it to be on this earth. We can become skeptical and cynical about life in general because we see so much bad and evil in our world. However, if we open our eyes, there are moments when we get a glimpse of real love. I've watched it closely in several of our senior adult couples over the last few years — couples who have weathered the storms of life and come out stronger and more in love.

James and Dot were that way. James recently turned ninety years old. He is a World War II veteran who began serving his country at the age of seventeen. Think about that for a moment. He and Dot became husband and wife over seventy years ago. In the last couple of years, due to their age and ailments, they've both been in the hospital. I've been present with them so many times and watched them hold hands and kiss each other from the side of a hospital bed. Dot told me a few months ago when James was in the Emergency Room: "You know he's my heart."

Two days ago, in their home, Dot went home to be with her Lord. James was at her side. Here is a gentleman who has handled life with grace and dignity. I watched him weep. Oh, how he loved her, and she loved him. He's doing well, for he knows their time of separation will be brief. Then their love will be perfect. I am honored I got to witness it on this earth. It gives one hope.

Godspeed my friends.

> *And now these three remain: faith, hope and love. But the greatest of these is love.*
>
> ~1 Corinthians 13:13 NIV

START HERE...

The Fault Finders

There are those in life who have become experts at pointing out the faults of others. However, these same individuals have a hard time seeing the shortcomings in their lives. It's so much easier to see how sorry other people are because it helps us justify, or even ignore, the mistakes we've made. However, I believe it was Jesus who asked: "Why do you look at the speck of sawdust in your brother's eye and pay no attention to the plank in your own eye?" (Matthew 7:3). But as long as we can judge others, we do not have to judge our own actions.

Let me make this clear. There is no big sin, little sin, or medium size sin. Sin is sin. The Bible teaches us: "for all have sinned and fall short of the glory of God" (Romans 3:23 NIV). That word "all" is inclusive – you, me, everyone. Over the years I've come to realize that I'm in no position to judge another person. That is God's job. I'm responsible for my actions and my attitude towards others. Those actions and attitudes will either have a positive or negative influence on the Kingdom.

When we become fault finders, we regress in our relationship with God. When we extend grace, forgiveness, and love, we demonstrate the very nature of God Himself. Be the best that you can be; life will become more meaningful, and you will have less time to talk about others.

Godspeed my friends.

> *Do not judge, or you too will be judged. For in the same way you judge others, you will be judged, and with the measure you use, it will be measured to you. Why do you look at the speck of sawdust in your brother's eye and pay no attention to the plank in your own eye? How can you say to your brother, "Let me take the speck out of your eye," when all the time there is a*

plank in your own eye? You hypocrite, first take the plank out of your own eye, and then you will see clearly to remove the speck from your brother's eye.

~Matthew 7:1-5 NIV

START HERE...

A Prayer for All of Us

Lord, we humbly come before your presence today and kneel before your throne. We acknowledge you are indeed the King of Kings and Lord of Lords. We realize You, and You alone, are holy and worthy of praise. We also understand that the message of salvation is as narrow as the cross, but your will for your children is as wide as the grace of God. We understand that we aren't worthy of your love and forgiveness, but you have provided us a way to come to you through your one and only Son, Jesus. And for that, we are eternally grateful. Lord, today many of us are struggling, and our faith is, at times, fragile. For some of us, our homes are a wreck; our family relationships are beaten up and torn apart at the seams. We aren't the husbands, wives, or children that you designed us to be; so, we're begging you to help us put the pieces back together. We know "unless the Lord builds a house, its laborers labor in vain." Father, some of us are struggling with financial troubles. No matter what we do, we can't seem to make ends meet. Remind us to make you our financial partner. Lord, heal our broken cities. Help us to see past color, race, and gender to realize we are all created in your image. God, there are many today who feel as though they aren't worthy of anyone's love. Remind them that you loved and valued them so much that you died for them.

Father, we pray for our nation in a very special way today. The evil one is laughing with great pleasure at the division he has caused. Help us to see past politics and opinions, and remember, you gave us this land and this life, and that you could also take it away at any second. Remind us that we can't love you and hate our brother or sister at the same time. Thank you, Lord Jesus, for loving me, for I echo the words of the Apostle Paul: "I am the chief of all sinners!" However, you love me and the rest of the world as we are and not as we ought to be. Bless us this day as we walk hand in hand with you. In the powerful name of Jesus, we pray. Amen; so let it be.

Godspeed my friends.

The Lord is far from the wicked, but he hears the prayer of the righteous.
~Proverbs 15:29 NIV

START HERE...

Acknowledgments

I want to thank my staff and fellow teammates at Pleasant Hill Baptist Church – Lisa Latham, Savannah Sloan, David Honeycutt, Franklin Denham, Allen Harris, and Ron Mumbower. All of you have blessed and enriched my life. It has been my highest honor to serve with all of you.

I want to thank my parents, Rev. and Mrs. James Albert Hurt, Sr., who taught me more about ministry than all my seminary courses combined. I am a living legacy to your life and ministry.

I want to express my gratitude to my friend, Toxey Hall, III, from Canton, Mississippi. Without your encouragement and support, this book would have still been just a dream. "Thank you" does not seem adequate, my friend.

I must thank Dr. Norman Shumate and Cynthia Wilkinson for editing the manuscript. Both of you spent countless hours making this book better than it otherwise would be. I never realized how little I knew about the English language until I got your corrections.

I also want to thank Ashley Bradberry for taking my picture. You made me look good!

I would be remiss if I did not say thanks to my family for their love and support. My daughters, Laura Jo and Melanie, have been my pride and joy since they entered the world. My daughters will always be "Daddy's girls," but they have also blessed me with two fantastic sons-in-law, Grant and Morgan. I can't imagine my life without all of you in it.

They say behind every good man is a good woman. That is true in my life. There is no way that I can adequately express my love and appreciation to Tommi Jo for standing firmly by my side for over thirty-five years. Through all the moves and transitions over the years you have always believed in my ministry and loved me in spite of myself.

Finally, to my soon-to-arrive grandson, Judson Miles Brashier, I have not met you, but you have already captured my heart. I cannot wait to spend time with you and spoil you rotten.